THE WAY
OF THE
WARRIOR

THE WAY OF THE WARRIOR

AN ANCIENT PATH TO INNER PEACE

ERWIN RAPHAEL McMANUS

BESTSELLING AUTHOR OF THE LAST ARROW

WATERBROOK

All Scripture quotations, unless otherwise indicated, are taken from the Holy Bible, New International Version®, NIV®. Copyright © 1973, 1978, 1984, 2011 by Biblica Inc.® Used by permission. All rights reserved worldwide. (www.zondervan.com). The "NIV" and "New International Version" are trademarks registered in the United States Patent and Trademark Office by Biblica Inc.™ Scripture quotations marked (KJV) are taken from the King James Version. Scripture quotations marked (NASB) are taken from the New American Standard Bible®, copyright © 1960, 1962, 1963, 1968, 1971, 1972, 1973, 1975, 1977, 1995 by the Lockman Foundation. Used by permission. (www.Lockman.org).

Details in some anecdotes and stories have been changed to protect the identities of the persons involved.

This book is not intended to replace the medical advice of a trained medical professional. Readers are advised to consult a physician or other qualified health-care professional regarding treatment of their medical problems. The author and publisher specifically disclaim liability, loss, or risk, personal or otherwise, which is incurred as a consequence, directly or indirectly, of the use or application of any of the contents of this book.

Copyright © 2019 by Erwin Raphael McManus
Discussion Questions copyright © 2021 by Erwin Raphael McManus

All rights reserved.

Published in the United States by WaterBrook, an imprint of Random House, a division of Penguin Random House LLC.

WATERBROOK® and its deer colophon are registered trademarks of Penguin Random House LLC.

Published in association with The Fedd Agency, Inc., P.O. Box 341973, Austin, TX 78734.

The snow story in chapter 7 is taken from *The Barbarian Way* by Erwin Raphael McManus. Copyright © 2005 by Erwin Raphael McManus. Used with permission of Thomas Nelson. www.thomasnelson.com

Trade Paperback ISBN 978-1-60142-958-2

The Library of Congress has cataloged the hardcover edition as follows:
Names: McManus, Erwin Raphael, author.
Title: The way of the warrior : an ancient path to inner peace / Erwin Raphael McManus.
Description: First edition. | New York : WaterBrook, 2019.
Identifiers: LCCN 2018038441 | ISBN 9781601429568 (hardcover) | ISBN 9781601429575 (electronic)
Subjects: LCSH: Peace of mind—Religious aspects—Christianity.
Classification: LCC BV4908.5 .M3575 2019 | DDC 248.4—dc23
LC record available at https://lccn.loc.gov/2018038441

Printed in the United States of America on acid-free paper

waterbrookmultnomah.com

2nd Printing

First Trade Paperback Edition

SPECIAL SALES Most WaterBrook books are available at special quantity discounts when purchased in bulk by corporations, organizations, and special-interest groups. Custom imprinting or excerpting can also be done to fit special needs. For information, please email specialmarketscms@penguinrandomhouse.com.

To Kim

There is no one else I could dedicate a book called
The Way of the Warrior than to you, my Love.
We have journeyed together for over thirty-five years, and from the days
of our youth we have traveled to unknown lands, walked into untold
mysteries, and chosen to live in absurd risk and unexpected adventure.
You personify courage and strength.
You defied the odds of birth and status.
You rose out of poverty and hardship.
You refused to allow how your story began to determine how it would end.
You chose a path that no one had walked before you.
You refused to surrender your dreams though no one
fought for you or with you.
You had the faith of a child and the valor of a warrior.
When you were afraid of the dark, it only made you walk
courageously into the light.
Yet you somehow knew that though you were alone,
you were not forgotten.
You carried your dreams with such passion and determination
that you were destined to live them.
You believed in a future no one else could see or even fathom.
You fought for your future.
Now you fight for the future of those who desperately need a heroine.
You journey the earth to find those who need to know that
they are not forgotten or alone.
You fight for love, and love is your greatest weapon.
Your path is the way of the warrior.
It has been my joy to have walked it with you.
People search their entire lives for what I have found in you.
You are the better side of me.
Always.

Contents

The Code of the Warrior

I t's probably not a good idea for a writer to reveal to his readers where his ideas come from, but in this case, I am making an exception. I could try to give you context, but I'm not sure I can fully explain what came to me—or maybe more precisely, how it came to me. I was driving through Los Angeles on a seemingly average day.

I should preface what I am about to say with the fact that I have a wildly vivid imagination that is informed by a lifetime of daydreaming. More often than not, I find myself in unexpected places, talking to people I'm fairly certain I have never met in real life but who feel very real to me. Sometimes I'm in the curious situation where my imagination takes the lead and I feel more like an innocent bystander.

So on that day as I was driving through Los Angeles, I suddenly heard a voice inside my head whispering a thought that had never occurred to me. I share it with you just as I heard it: *The warrior is not ready for battle until they have come to know peace. This is the way of the warrior.* What I heard felt like more than just an insight; it felt like an invitation. And this invitation, as strange as it sounds, was the beginning of this book.

The words were not without personality. It was as if I somehow dropped into an ancient time. I could see the warrior's face and every wrinkle that defined a lifetime of both struggle and wisdom. In that moment, I had been transplanted to sixteenth-century Japan and was listening to the counsel of an ancient samurai trying to teach his young apprentice the difference between the way of violence and the way of the warrior.

It's easy enough for me to understand some of the experiences that had informed this moment in my imagination. Probably my favorite film of all time is the *Seven Samurai,* written and directed by Akira Kurosawa. The movie is set in sixteenth-century Japan, where farmers from a small village are being oppressed by a band of roving bandits. It's a story about how one retired samurai, long past his prime, gathers together six other samurai to help him defend this poor village. This film came out four years before I was born, and although I grew up without a knowledge of all the heroes written about in the Bible, it was stories like this one that placed within me a heroic narrative. Throughout my life, I have always admired the courage and honor of Kambei Shimada, the first of the seven samurai.

It was years later that I sat mesmerized watching for the fourth or fifth time the 2002 release of the Chinese film *Hero.* Through the breathtaking cinematography, I felt transported into the world of a hero whose name is literally Nameless. I had a similar experience only a year later as the only person in a theater who could not speak Chinese, watching the premiere of *Crouching Tiger, Hidden*

Dragon. And I must confess that the year after that I was deeply impressed by the elegance and profundity of Ken Watanabe's performance as Katsumoto in *The Last Samurai.*

Each of these stories wove a heroic narrative within my soul and reminded me that there is a significant difference between violence and honor, between revenge and courage, between the way of war and the way of the warrior.

Perhaps these films and the endless number of narratives that have formed my imagination allowed me to hear the first line of this book as if it called to me from ancient times, but I know it was more than that. My thoughts were also informed by the realities that we face every day in our present times. We live in a world that seems to be marked and defined by senseless violence. We now have a generation whose only impression of human history is an era of global terrorism. Our children can no longer go to school with the assumption of safety but must live with the imminent threat of a senseless massacre taking place on any given day. From Islamic extremists to white supremacists, hate seems to be the order of the day. I still struggle to grasp the kind of rage, hate, and violence that drives a person to walk into a school with more ammunition than a military specialist and senselessly take innocent lives.

It seems pretty clear to me there is something terribly wrong in our world. I, like so many others, long for peace. I would give anything to see the end of violence. Where wars once seemed solely the concern of soldiers, we now know that the problem runs much deeper than places on maps "over there."

I have been asked many times over the years why the Bible depicts God as a God of war. You can't escape the fact that there are many battles recorded in Scripture. In the ancient world, the language of war was very common, and for many ancient peoples it was almost interwoven into the language of faith. I am always reminded that it is not God who created humanity to live in violence, but rather it is humanity that chooses violence. That is our history. That is our present, both as a species and as individuals. We would have a history of even more wars if God did not exist. Our past is one of conflict, of division, of greed and power—a constant battle where nation rises up against nation, and brother rises up against brother.

This is not the history of God; this is the history of us. God is tainted by being part of our story, but the story of God is a story of peace. What does the story of peace look like when it's dropped into the middle of a humanity that knows only conflict and violence? The language of God as a warrior came to exist because he intervened for the defenseless. He heard the cries of a people battling slavery and came to set them free. So yes, it was a declaration of war against injustice, oppression, and inhumanity.

It was Cain who killed Abel. It was God who held Cain accountable and yet still protected him from further violence. It would be easy to blame God for what we have created and to impugn his character because he works to bring peace into our stories rather than manipulating every aspect of the story from the outset. I have become convinced that, more than any of us, God understands the war that rages within and around us and that he longs to lead us to the end of violence. We are people of war because we are a people at war. All the violence we see in the world is but a small glimpse of the violence that churns in us. This war that rages within us eventually boils over and sets the world on fire.

It is the war within us that is the focus of *The Way of the Warrior*. I choose this imagery because I am convinced that the only path toward world peace is inner peace. Even as I write this book, I am surrounded by an endless number of people—people I love, people I care deeply about—who struggle with inner demons that put them at daily risk. Suicide has become a global epidemic even among the educated and affluent. Those who would seem to have the most reasons to live can't think of even one.

Depression is at an epidemic level, and we can't seem to design medication fast enough to keep us from drowning in an abyss that exists within us. Otherwise talented, gifted, and extraordinary human beings are paralyzed by anxiety and overwhelmed by stress. And a growing number of young men and women who have never gone to war find themselves in a battle with post-traumatic stress disorder.

The sudden outbreaks of violence that have marked the history of our children can no longer be seen as an anomaly and must be addressed as a cultural state of emergency. I am tired of losing people I love. We cannot sit idly by, hoping that the problems will somehow self-correct. Maybe I can't bring peace on earth by writing this book, but if I can bring peace to one person, I will consider my job done.

Our only hope for societal peace is inner peace, and inner peace will not come without a battle. The struggle is real. The battle lines have been drawn, and it is a battle for our souls. I chose the language of *The Way of the Warrior* not because I desire to romanticize war but because I hope to help us find a pathway to peace. This war must be won one person at a time, one heart at a time, one life at a time.

This, by the way, is the way of Jesus. This is how he came to bring peace on earth. While others hoped he would call out an army, incite a rebellion, and use his power to topple an empire, he chose a different way. He did not surrender to the status quo nor succumb to the inevitable rule of oppressive powers. He had absolute confidence that his revolution would prevail. He knew the way to peace. He understood the source of all wars. He knew it all began in the human heart.

It is the way of Jesus that is the ancient path to inner peace. In choosing to follow him, I have chosen the way of the warrior. Every day I find myself at war. Even after all these years there are battles that rage within me. But rather than losing ground, I find myself gaining it day by day. I am still fighting behind enemy lines. I have known all the enemies of the human spirit. I have known fear and doubt; I have known bitterness and anger; I have known jealousy and greed. They are all too familiar to me. And after many years of walking this ancient path, I have come to know this one truth most certainly: the world within you will create the world around you.

Inner peace does not come by accident, nor by desire. Inner

peace is a journey toward self-mastery. The way of the warrior is a discipline of the soul. It is a journey toward enlightenment. And ultimately it is the outcome of a relationship with the Creator of the universe. The world in which Jesus lived never knew peace, yet no matter how hard the powerful tried, they could never steal his peace. It should not surprise us that it was an act of violence that became for us our way to peace. The cross points the way, but we must choose the path. The Bible speaks of darkness and light, reminding us there is a war that rages within us all.

Have you surrendered to the darkness? Have you lost sight of the light? Have you found yourself exhausted by the struggle yet somehow you refused to give up on the fight? You are not alone. The battle that rages within you was never meant to be fought alone. And if you feel as if you are one breath from giving up, I hope somehow I can convince you that the God who created you is fighting for you.

You cannot give up on yourself when God considers you worth the fight. The cross upon which Jesus died will never be known as a symbol of defeat or a declaration of surrender. The cross will be forever remembered, long after time ceases to exist, not just as a declaration of the one who stands victorious but as a promise that in the end war will surrender to peace. It is the way of Jesus that is the ancient path to inner peace. His life is the way of the warrior.

The Warrior Fights Only for Peace

The warrior is not ready for battle until they have come to know peace. For all the wars that have ever been waged from the beginning of time were first born in a person's heart. We have a history of war because our souls are at war. We have conflicts because our hearts are conflicted. Every war, every conflict, every act of violence exists because our souls rage. Our only hope for peace is to win the battle within. Every war against another is a war that never should have been fought. It should have been won long before. It should have been won from within. This is our first battle. The war to end all wars is the battle for the human heart. This is the war we must win. To know peace is the way of the warrior.

It is impossible to ignore that God is often associated with wars. Certainly the people of Israel have a history of war as well as one of faith. We might conclude that the God of Scripture is a God of war, yet the opposite is true. God is a God of peace. We are the ones who brought war to the human story. And since then, God has been fighting for us to find our way back to peace.

Solomon tells us that there is a time for war and a time for peace.[1] Our history betrays us though. Our past is marked by war, whereas peace has forever eluded us. Sadly, the story of humanity can be marked by the weapons we have forged. From stones to arrows to swords to bullets to missiles, our inventions betray our intentions. An outside observer might say that we are creatures of violence for whom peace is simply the language of poets and philosophers. Yet the way of the warrior is not about refining our skills for war; it is about choosing the path of peace.

I have chosen this language, but you may find it at first contrary to the intention of this book. Peace can come only when it is fought for. This is true for any and every kind of peace, whether it's peace on earth, interpersonal peace, or inner peace. It never comes to the passive. In fact, if you choose the way of peace, you will find yourself in a constant struggle and endless battle. The peace we seek must come from within, and this, you will discover, is the greatest of all battles. It was Job who uttered, "What I feared has come upon me; what I dreaded has happened to me. I have no peace, no quietness; I have no rest, but only turmoil."[2]

I am convinced his words echo in every heart: "I have no peace, no quietness; I have no rest, but only turmoil." It is a story that all of us can write. It is the struggle that all of us know, some more profoundly than others.

If precedent is an accurate predictor of the future, we should not expect we will ever know a world defined by peace. It is perplexing when I meet people who believe there is no God and yet still believe in peace. After all, peace is an ideal of which we speak, but it's something this world has never fully known. The human story is marked by envy, jealousy, greed, violence, and bloodshed. There will never be peace on earth until there is peace in us. This is why the way of the warrior must begin here. To find your strength you must find your peace, for the path to inner strength is inner peace.

This is where our journey begins. The way of the warrior begins with finding the missing *peace*. There are certain names that stand out throughout history as beacons of peace. Strangely, when you choose the path of peace in the midst of violence and rage, you are often simply remembered by a single name—for example, Gandhi, Mandela, Teresa, Tutu, Buddha, and, of course, Jesus. Although each of them advocated for peace in the midst of violence, it is Jesus alone who claimed to actually be the peace our souls long for.

Jesus lived in a time of turmoil and conflict. He was born in a world where his people were oppressed by a foreign empire. Although we think of Jesus as a man born free, he was actually born a slave. In fact, Jesus was a survivor of an infanticide ordered by a king who feared for his reign. All of Israel lived enslaved by the Roman Empire. Israel belonged to Rome. The Hebrews were the Romans' possession. As a man, Jesus was considered a subject to a Caesar who proclaimed himself a god with the right to rule over the lives of all mankind. If Jesus knew freedom, it was not because of his circumstance. If Jesus knew peace, it was in contrast to the chaos that surrounded him. It is in this context that he spoke to his disciples and said to them, "Peace I leave with you; my peace I give you. I do not give to you as the world gives. Do not let your hearts be troubled and do not be afraid."[3]

Jesus's words must have seemed both profound and perplexing to those who heard them. After all, they expected him to bring peace. Many who believed he was the Messiah thought that he would come to deliver them from the Roman Empire. The title *Messiah* had come to mean something very specific to the Jewish people. They expected that this Messiah would parallel the life of King David. It would be this Messiah that would lead his people to overthrow the greatest empire in the world. This Messiah would become their king, and the fulfillment of the promise would be found in their freedom. The coming of the Messiah would be the end of oppression.

The words of Isaiah had been passed on for generations: "Of the greatness of his government and peace there will be no end. He will reign on David's throne and over his kingdom, establishing and upholding it with justice and righteousness from that time on and forever."[4]

There was a very simple litmus test for the Messiah: if he does not establish peace, he cannot be the Messiah. It was his responsibility to bring them peace; he was the embodiment of true peace, yet the type of peace they had hoped for never came. His words must have seemed bittersweet. He spoke of peace with such certainty in the midst of such chaos that it probably caused many onlookers to assume Jesus was a bit naive. There must have been many who wanted to look at Jesus and say, "As hopeful and poetic as your words may be, you need to get a grip on reality. This is not peace. If you came to set us free, to establish a kingdom of peace, then you are a dismal failure and a grave disappointment to all of us who have been waiting so long for the Messiah to bring about change."

No one had quite the courage to speak so bluntly to Jesus, but there couldn't have been anything more frustrating for Jesus's listeners than a declaration of peace when their world was in turmoil. Even today, Jesus's words cut to the very depth of our souls, and he seems to know our thoughts even as he speaks peace into our lives: "I do not give to you as the world gives." It's almost as if in one quick phrase he indicts the history of human violence. The peace he brings will never come to us the way we had hoped or expected. This is not the way of the warrior, only the way of violence.

You might find it peculiar that I would describe Jesus as a warrior. After all, he is most commonly known as a man of peace. Yet you cannot properly understand Jesus if you do not grasp that his entire life's purpose was to win the greatest battle of the greatest war that has ever been fought.

God stepped into human history to fight for us. He did not hope for peace; he fought for peace. Sometimes the true mission of Jesus is misunderstood because he never carried a physical weapon in his hands. Yet if you want to see the true marks of a warrior, you need to look at the scars on his hands. In his death and resurrection,

Jesus took upon himself all the violence of the world so he could bring all the world his peace. That is why he is most profoundly and uniquely the warrior of peace. That is why we're pursuing his path.

The War Within

Jesus tells us, "Do not let your hearts be troubled and do not be afraid."[5] With simplicity and wisdom, he cuts between the two things that steal our peace, for the greatest enemies of the peace within are worry and fear.

All around me I find troubled hearts—men and women drowning in worry. We have become so adept at worrying that we have created an endless number of names to describe the nuances. Whether we use the language of stress or anxiety or find ourselves in the depths of depression or despair, worry is the source of so much of our hearts' troubles. Worry projects a negative view of the world around us. Worry projects a negative future. Worry is an act of faith. It is a deep-seated belief in worst-case scenarios. Worry is not rooted in reality but does affect our reality.

I've also found irony in these words of Paul: "Be anxious for nothing."[6] I know that what he means is that we should not allow anything to make us anxious, but the truth is that it is usually *nothing* that is making us anxious. Our anxiety, our distress, our worry—when stripped to its very essence—is rooted in nothing, or at least in nothing we can control. Paul's solution, of course, is to be anxious in nothing, but in all things, through prayer, we should bring our thanksgiving to God.[7] It seems he's telling us that anxiety comes when we try to control things that are out of our control. We become anxious because we haven't learned to trust.

It is interesting that in another place where Jesus speaks of peace, he brings up trouble once more. Here he says to his disciples, "I have told you these things, so that in me you may have peace. In this world you will have trouble."[8]

This is an important contrast. First he says to us, "Do not let your hearts be troubled," but then he says to us, "In this world you will have trouble." We have no control over the reality that in this world we will have trouble, but we have control over whether we decide to allow our hearts to be troubled. He makes the promise that though there will be trouble in this world, we can take heart, for he has overcome the world. Our worry will steal our peace, and when peace is missing, we find ourselves drowning in anxiety and crumbling under the weight of life's pressures.

He also said, "Do not be afraid." If worry wars against our peace, fear is perhaps an even greater foe. When we live our lives afraid, it creates turmoil and chaos within us. Fear is the enemy of peace. While worry will rob our joy, fear will steal our freedom, for what we fear establishes the boundaries of our freedom. What we fear has mastery over our souls. When we are anxious, we lose our strength. When we are afraid, we lose our courage. When we have found peace, we have both the strength and courage to live the lives we were created to live.

Even in my own life, I see the relationship between worry, anxiety, and the inability to control the world around me. Throughout my life I have had a fear of dogs. Even to this day I still jump when a dog moves in my direction, even though I love dogs. The root of this fear is not undiagnosable for me.

When I was around five years old, I saw my brother get bitten by a dog. It could have been either one of us, but as life would have it, he was the one the dog targeted. Oddly enough, my brother, who was actually bitten by the dog, never developed any fear of dogs whatsoever. My fear and anxiety were rooted in what could have happened and not in the reality of what did happen. It was as if for the rest of my life I kept waiting for what I feared to happen, even though to this day I have never been bitten by a dog.

For years I was afraid of roller coasters. Again, it was not rooted in something irrational. When I was around ten years old, the seat belt broke while I was riding a roller coaster, and I held on for my dear life. I remember screaming my guts out, trying to get the operator's attention, but he was too busy smoking to notice. I was never thrown out of the roller coaster, as I managed to hold on until it finally came to a stop, but out of that negative experience an enduring fear took over. I spent years watching other people ride roller coasters. But that's exactly what fear and anxiety do to you: they put you on the sideline watching life happen. I couldn't control the variables if I got into the roller coaster, so I stayed on solid ground to give me a sense of control.

It was years later when I finally determined to overcome that fear. Without fully understanding the complex nature of fear and anxiety, I knew what I had to do was get on a roller coaster. I had to destroy an ingrained belief that if I got on the coaster I would die. Since that time, I have enjoyed a lifetime of extreme inclines and insane drops. I love roller coasters. I love the feeling that happens when my stomach drops. I love the illusion of free-falling and plummeting to my death.

Ironically, those two phobias in my life helped me establish a pattern of overcoming fears in multiple arenas. Every fear feels justified. One reason is that every fear has a seed of truth in it. But the thing is that you do not ultimately have control over your life. Peace does not come because you finally have control over your life; peace comes when you no longer need control.

If fear has a direct object, anxiety is fear without an object. We experience anxiety when we feel overwhelmed by life. In order to reduce our anxiety, we often create smaller and smaller boundaries to give us some sense of control over our lives.

The Strength of Peace

The warrior's strength is their peace. Jesus did not come to conquer kingdoms or nations; he came to conquer hearts and minds. If you are going to walk in the way of Jesus, you must know that you are to enter darkness that desperately needs the light. In describing the path that John the Baptist would prepare for Jesus of Nazareth, these words were spoken about John at his birth by his father, Zechariah:

"You will go on before the Lord to prepare the way for him, to give his people the knowledge of salvation through the forgiveness of their sins, because of the tender mercy of our God, by which the rising sun will come to us from heaven to shine on those living in darkness and in the shadow of death, to guide our feet into the path of peace."[9]

The path of peace comes only when we're willing to walk into our own darkness and face our own shadows. We must face the very things that steal our peace from us whether they are born out of our fear or our doubts. The concept of peace is deeply rooted in the history that shaped the world and culture of Jesus's day. The Hebrew word for "peace" is *shalom*. The word *shalom* is layered, complex, and elegant in its nuances. At its most superficial level, *shalom* is basically used as a form of greeting. In many ways it can be compared with the English word *goodbye,* which is simply a part of our common language but is rooted in the phrase "God be with you."

Shalom is a greeting with deep implications. It is most commonly translated and understood to mean "peace," but the peace of shalom is rich in its textures. The word extends beyond meaning "peace" to meaning "harmony, wholeness, completeness, prosperity, welfare, and tranquility."[10] To experience shalom is to find wholeness. When we find peace, we are made whole. The ultimate goal of peace is that we not only are made whole within ourselves but also become part of the whole within all of creation. The very concept of shalom assumes that the original intention of God is for all things to be interconnected—that when there is peace, there is relationship and harmony between all things.

The clearest evidence that we lack peace is that we all sense a tearing between us, a separation that divides us from God, from our true selves, and from others, and yes, even creation. The evidence that peace is missing is the break between us and God, the violence of brother against brother, and our destruction of and irresponsibility with the creation we have been entrusted with. When there is peace, all these relationships are made right and everything is made whole. When we are broken, all we are left with are the pieces of our true selves.

As much evidence as there is around us that we desperately need to find our peace, there is even deeper proof within us of how peace has eluded us. When our hearts have not found peace, we become filled with the darkest expressions of ourselves. We're filled with not only fear and doubt but also greed and envy, anger and bitterness, loneliness and disconnection, despair and hopelessness. Each of these are external forces that war against our inner worlds.

We struggle with envy because we want the life that isn't ours.

We struggle with greed because we want to possess what is not ours to have.

We struggle with feelings of insignificance because we have made our worth dependent on the opinions of others.

We struggle with identity because we don't know who we are outside of what we do.

We struggle with loneliness because we are searching for love rather than giving it.

We will never know peace as long as we are slaves to external forces of the world and create our identities from the outside in. We will never know peace if we lose the present because we are trapped in the past and paralyzed by the future. This is in no small part why we live in a culture crippled by depression and anxiety. Depression is rooted in your past; anxiety is rooted in your imagined future.

Depression is how your soul processes regret; anxiety is how your soul processes fear.

Depression traps you in your worst and most painful memories; anxiety imagines your worst and most painful future.

You lose the present when you hide from your past and run from your future. Depression and anxiety convince you that the past is your future and so the future must be avoided at all costs. Scripture tells us to "be anxious for nothing, but in everything by prayer and supplication with thanksgiving let your requests be made known to God."[11]

It was intended for us to be fully present in the moment. Only the present will free you from the past, and only the present will free you to your future. The path to freedom from your past and freedom to your future is the connectedness that comes from living this moment fully present. It may seem strange, but you connect to the transcendent only when you are fully present. When you experience God's presence in the moment, the moment becomes eternal.

Be here right now.

The path of peace comes not from the outside in but from the inside out. Here's how Isaiah described the path toward peace: "You will keep in perfect peace those whose minds are steadfast, because they trust in you."[12]

This is the path to mindfulness. This is the way to peace of mind. Not a journey to nothingness, but a journey to fullness. It is God who gives us perfect peace. More specifically, it is Jesus who has come to bring us this peace that our souls long for.

Forceful Peace

John the Baptist was chosen to prepare the way for the coming of Jesus. His mission was "to shine on those living in darkness and in the shadow of death, to guide our feet into the path of peace."[13]

The last thing anyone would ever say to describe John the Baptist is that he was compliant or even cooperative. John was a nonconformist in every way. His message was confrontational, and his very nature was forceful and powerful. Yet we are told that even his harsh tone and stark language were chosen for our own good. His purpose was to awaken those living in the darkness of the shadow of death and show that there is light and life available for all of us. It would be easy to see John as a man of war, yet his sole intent was to guide our feet into the path of peace.

Recently I heard my son, Aaron, explain that God goes to war only for the purpose of peace. Remember, John came only to prepare us for Jesus. To follow Jesus is to choose the path of peace. Everywhere he reigns, there is peace. When he was born, the declaration of the angelic beings was "Glory to God in the highest heaven, and on earth peace to those on whom his favor rests."[14] Through the most violent instrument of death the world has ever known, Jesus came to be our peace—yes, not to simply *bring* us peace but to *be* our peace.

When Aaron was in high school, I got a call letting me know that he was in danger of being expelled for getting in a fight. I had never known my son to be violent, so I was a little surprised. But when I discovered what was happening, it made perfect sense to me. Apparently, there was a cluster of kids who were physically abusive to a specific group of outsiders. Their hostility had become an every-day occurrence at Aaron's school. In this particular situation, there was a group of well-off white students bullying underprivileged Hispanic students.

One day Aaron felt he needed to intervene. He jumped into the fray to try to protect a classmate who was outnumbered and over-powered. More often than not, when you attempt to become a peacemaker, you become a target. After that day, Aaron became the focus of some redirected violence and anger.

The administration's stance was not helpful. Their advice for Aaron was that because he was the focus of the bullies' aggression, he would just need to fight back and defend himself. Yet when I asked what the consequences would be for taking such action, I was told that my son would be expelled if he fought back. You can imagine my confusion and frustration.

It's amazing how quickly you can go from peacemaker to hav-ing a reputation for violence. This is exactly the dilemma for God, who in the Old Testament is constantly depicted as a God of war and violence. The way it is told, he is both the Creator of war and an instigator of violence. The reality is that we are the ones who introduced violence to the human story. We are the ones who carry war in our hearts. God has literally tainted his reputation by determining to bring peace in the midst of our violence. If the world were at peace, God would not disrupt it with war. It is because the world is at war that God disrupts it to bring peace. The only reason God is at war is that he is fighting for us. Yes, God is a warrior—he is a warrior of peace. God will always fight for the good and the beautiful and the true.

God is not a God of war; God is a God of peace. When we are at war, we live beneath God's intention for us. The wars of humanity war against God's purpose in the world. The God of peace will not sit idly by and watch us destroy each other. He will not lose us to our own violence without a fight. We often blame God for involving himself in the wars of men, yet the reality is that for him to engage in human history, he had to enter into our violence and fight for peace. And peace on earth is worth the fight.

Jesus knows the condition of the human heart and that because of our condition we would always face conflicts and there would always be suffering. He knew the standards of this world had fallen far beneath the intention of the Father for all humanity, so he called us to a new way. He called us to choose peace as our power.

Jesus went on to say, "If anyone wants to sue you and take your shirt, hand over your coat as well."[15] As if it were not hard enough to choose peace over retaliation, Jesus also wants us to return greed with generosity. It seems that by now we would have learned that violence cannot be ended with violence, but I think few of us have ever realized that only generosity can overcome greed.

Many times we feel powerless when someone has taken something from us. It's easy to feel that the only way to reclaim our
power is to take what was lost and even more in return. Yet Jesus
calls us to a different way. No one can steal what you freely give
away. Live your life with open hands. Give away more than another
can take from you. As Jesus told his disciples, "If anyone forces you
to go one mile, go with them two miles."[16]

He challenged them, "I tell you, do not resist an evil person. If
anyone slaps you on the right cheek, turn to them the other cheek
also."[17] This was not a call to be powerless but to find a greater power
than returning evil for evil. It takes great strength to turn the other
cheek. Turning the other cheek means you took the blunt force
trauma of someone's worst and remained standing.

This is not the way of the weak; this is the way of the warrior.
This is a call to rise above our most primal instincts, let go of revenge and retaliation, and not be fooled into believing that anger is
a source of power. The warrior chooses honor and integrity and will
not lower themselves to the standard of those who would bring
them down to their level.

The imagery of turning the other cheek was abundantly clear to
Jesus's first-century Hebrew audience. Often their Roman captors
would slap them or strike them to try to elicit an angry response. If
any of them actually hit a Roman soldier, it would have cost the
captive his life. Only restraint would keep someone from falling
into that sort of trap.

It takes people of great strength to show restraint and trust that
God will be their protector. However, in addition to withstanding

abuse at the Roman soldier's hand, Jesus's listeners had to be wary of their own people. Some of the first-century Hebrews who stood in alliance with the Roman Empire would wrongfully sue their neighbors for the purpose of financial gain. This created further division in a time of great discord and made enemies of their own people. Now Jesus was giving them an unexpected strategy to end the enmity between their own families and friends. Give away more than you're being sued for—this would've been an unheard-of strategy.

Perhaps the greatest indignity in that day was when a Roman soldier would force a young Hebrew to carry the pack that his horse could easily handle. The Romans often thought of the Hebrews as nothing more than horses or dogs. They were not seen as truly human. Legally, Roman soldiers were empowered to make Hebrews carry their packs for a mile. Afterward they would release them back to daily activities in humiliation. Jesus gave his listeners an unexpected way to claim their strength, to reclaim their power, to proclaim their freedom: "If anyone forces you to carry their pack one mile, you carry it for two." Choose service over obligation, servanthood over slavery. If they force you to work, then confound them with a greater wisdom. Never forget that you are always free to do more.

Know Your Power

The way of peace is not a call to passivism. The way of peace is not a call to powerlessness. The way of peace is a call to know one's power. Jesus drove the money changers out of the temple. The Bible tells us he made a whip out of cords, overturned their tables, and drove them out. He would not allow them to leave with the money that they had gained.[18]

We rarely think of Jesus as physically imposing. He is most often depicted as a passive idealist rather than a warrior of peace. Yet in the cleansing of the temple, we are reminded that Jesus knew that peace would not come without a battle and it would not come without a cost. The way of peace is not for the weak or the weak of heart. The warrior knows their power, and they know their greatest weapon is peace. And with as many wars that will ever rage around us, the greatest battle for peace will always be within us. Every battle is first fought within. Jesus was never powerless. He was the epitome of controlled strength. Although he was always meek, he was never weak. He knew his power but never abused it.

The warrior knows that peace does not come from control but from relinquishing control. Everything in life that you try to control that is outside your control will steal from you your peace. You must choose to take hold of what you can control and let go of what you cannot.

You cannot control your circumstances, but you can control your character.

You cannot control the actions of others, but you can control the choices you make.

You cannot control the outcome, but you can control the process.

The battle for peace requires that you both take control and relinquish control. Peace of mind does not come because you have eliminated uncertainty but because you have clarity about what is important. Peace comes when you stop trying to control the world around you and instead take responsibility for the world within you. Inner peace is interconnected to your confidence in future possibilities. In other words, peace is intimately connected to hope. Peace is lost when you are drowning in worst-case scenarios. Peace of mind is not about certainty but about hope-filled mystery.

The warrior has peace of mind because they know that there is always a way to find light, even in the midst of the greatest darkness. They know that there is always hope to be found, even in despair. Peace can exist in the midst of turmoil only if you believe in the beauty of the future. Peace sees the beauty everywhere. When you walk in peace, you are overwhelmed by the wonder of the universe and the beauty of life.

The Battle Within

It was December 15, 2016, when my wife, Kim, and I sat in a doctor's office and heard him say that I had cancer. In fact, it was while writing my previous book, *The Last Arrow,* that we received this ominous news. I finished that book wondering if it would be my last. The weight of your words hits you much harder when you know that they may be your last.

On January 15, 2017, I shared publicly for the first time about my personal battle, and I must tell you it's not easy to fight a private battle in the public eye. It all happened so quickly. For a long time I had known there was something wrong with me, but it didn't truly feel real until it was diagnosed. It's kind of ironic, if you think about it, that you could have cancer eating away your body and you're never afraid because you don't know it's there. Is it the cancer that is so terrifying, or is it the knowledge of it?

You never know how you're going to react. I certainly had no idea what those days would be like for me. It would be two days later, on January 17, that I would admit myself to Huntington Memorial Hospital and allow the surgeons to do their best to save my life. I remember sharing with my family that I was giving myself permission to feel whatever I needed to feel. There was no time to pretend and no reason to waste what might be my last days by hiding from my deepest feelings, which would in essence lock out those I loved the most. If you're not honest with yourself, you cannot be honest with anyone else. When we close ourselves off from our inner pain and struggles, we inevitably close ourselves off to everyone in our lives as well.

I decided that if I felt anger, I was going to be angry. If I felt afraid, I was going to feel afraid. I was just going to let myself be human. I felt certain it would be okay with God and that he would understand if I fell short of the expectations of others.

Yet the strangest thing happened: I never felt anger, I never felt bitterness, and I never felt fear. After all, how could I be angry when I have lived such an extraordinary life? How could I be bitter when

I have known far more than my fair share of goodness? Still, with all that, what surprised me most was that I didn't feel afraid. I knew that it would be perfectly acceptable—in fact, expected—to be afraid. I even began to wonder if there was something wrong with me because I didn't feel fear. My greatest discovery in facing cancer was that I had actually come to know peace. And while I can tell you with absolute certainty that the source of that peace was without question Jesus, I would be remiss if I did not also say that the process to finding that peace was not quite that simple. The way of the warrior is in large part the journey toward coming to know that kind of peace. I am convinced that many people have lost their faith in God because they have confused source with process. Yes, God is the source of all peace, and that source is available to all of us freely. The process, though, requires struggle and resilience and does not come without a cost.

Now, don't get me wrong. I felt a sadness of the potential loss, not of the loss of my life but of the things I would not get to share in. I wanted to spend more years with my beautiful wife, Kim. I wanted to watch my son, Aaron, get married one day, hopefully— please, God! I wanted to live long enough to watch him flourish and step into the full strength of his gifts of leadership. I wanted to watch his children grow up and bring him immeasurable joy. I wanted to be here to see my daughter, Mariah, and her husband, Jake, flourish in their careers; watch their music travel across the world; and hopefully one day watch them have kids of their own. There are so many things in this life that I love, and they would have been hard to say goodbye to. But that's different than fear. Fear is crippling and steals your life from you. Fear is the enemy of peace.

The surgery was supposed to last two hours, but it lasted more than six. My surgeon explained that part of what took so long was the extent of the cancer and the unexpected work of removing a large amount of scar tissue from when my appendix had ruptured when I was a young boy. Imagine finding out forty-six years after the fact that your appendix had burst when you were twelve years old.

All I remember from being that age is turmoil. I remember being completely disconnected from the world around me. I remember when my parents, not knowing how to help me, found me professional counseling. I remember going in and out of both a psychiatric office and a hospital for a battery of tests that could find nothing wrong with me. They decided to do exploratory surgery. I was told that the cause of my pain was psychosomatic and, in the end, that there had been nothing wrong with me.

I never knew that two surgeries more than forty years apart would somehow be so interconnected. I spent the better part of forty years believing there had been nothing wrong with me, that the surgery was a waste of time, that the pain was all in my head. The surgery to remove only my cancer also became the surgery that removed the scar tissue that had been there for more than four decades.

There was for me a strange irony in learning that there *had* actually been something physically wrong with me. I had always thought it was only psychological, but it turned out not to be all in my head. I had lived more than forty years with scars that I did not know were there, yet those were not the scars that left me damaged. There were much deeper scars than could ever be caused by a surgeon's knife. Somewhere early in my life, way younger than should ever happen to anyone, my soul found itself in disarray.

I don't know when it happened, but early in my life, I lost my peace. Most of my memories of childhood are filled with nightmares, with an overwhelming sense of despair and anxiety. There wasn't really language for it back then, but I was in a fight for my life, as I was drowning in depression and hopelessness. So you cannot know how unexpected it was that in facing cancer, I felt none of those things that I'd felt so profoundly when I was much younger and more fragile. I can tell you that it is more than a theory and more than an aspiration. Not only can you know peace, but you can also be at peace. And while the world around you rages, the world within you can know a strange stillness and an unexpected calm.

Stand in Your Pain

It was around 9:00 p.m. when I was finally wheeled into my hospital room to begin my recovery after surgery. The surgical procedure had required that six holes pierce the area around my abdomen while a robot called "da Vinci" carved away the cancerous cells and ensured that it left all the healthy organs intact. It was almost precisely three hours later, at the stroke of midnight, that I woke up and decided I would take a walk. I woke up my wife and asked her to help me get out of the bed. She was uncooperative, to put it mildly, so I buzzed the nurse and informed her that I was ready to get out of bed and begin the process of rehabilitation.

Both my wife and the nurse insisted this was a bad idea—that I had just come out of six hours of surgery and needed to give myself time to heal. So I asked the nurse point blank, "Is there really any more damage I could do if I got out of bed and started walking?" She conceded that there was nothing harmful about walking, but it would be terribly painful. So I insisted, and my mind would not be changed.

Then the nurse moved to a second strategy. If she couldn't keep me in bed, she at the very least needed to make sure I was medicated. She encouraged me to give her a few moments to get some painkillers into my system so I would not be overwhelmed by the pain. For some reason my mind was so clear. I looked at her and explained that the whole point was to feel pain—that I would not allow her to give me painkillers. I understood that this might be more pain than I could bear. I went on to explain that I knew that if I could bear this pain, I could bear whatever pain was ahead of me, so reluctantly the nurse and my wife helped me out of the bed.

I stood to my feet, and I think in this case it would be literal to say I wanted to scream my guts out. The first step was unbearable, the second step even more. The third and fourth steps were unrelenting, the fifth and sixth unforgiving. I wish I could tell you that God somehow intervened in that moment and made me oblivious to the pain, but if anything, the gift God gave me was to make me more aware of it. I stood in the middle of my pain. I stepped into my pain. I walked through my pain. You see, one thing I was certain of was that on the other side of my pain, there awaited my freedom.

So many of us see pain as the boundary of our limitations. When we experience pain, that's when we choose to stop. We have confused knowing peace with becoming prisoners. The way of peace is not without pain. The way of peace comes only by walking through the pain.

I'll never forget walking out of that room with a catheter attached to my body and walking for a few minutes down that hallway until what once felt unbearable was now just a part of who I was. Three hours later I made myself get up again and walk farther than I had before. By eight o'clock in the morning, when I noticed that there was a nurse shift change, I got myself out of my bed, grabbed my clothes, went and took a shower, and dressed myself to leave. By the time my wife returned from taking a small break, I was dressed and ready to go. It took a lot of negotiating to get released from the hospital, since in the nurses' minds I was still a patient. But I would not be their prisoner. I had to walk through my pain, and I was ready to walk free.

Some time has passed since I walked out those doors, and frankly, when I write about having cancer, it feels as if I am talking about someone else's life. Since that time, I have met so many people who have gone through similar challenges far worse than my own.

And since my battle with cancer, I have had an endless number of battles of different kinds. This one thing remains true: right behind the battle that has just been fought, another battle lies in wait.

For every war that you've bled for and won, there is another war waiting to overtake you. There is no path in this life where you can escape those things that will war against your peace. Even Jesus, the Prince of Peace, knew that his path would lead him to agony and suffering. Even for Jesus, there was no escape from the war that rages within the human spirit. Yet in the most violent moment of his life, when he carried the sins of the world upon himself on the cross amidst brutality, he made the way for us to know peace. This is the way of the warrior—not that we run from our suffering, not that we shrink back from the sacrifices demanded of us, but that in the midst of it, regardless of what rages around us, we are at peace.

Jesus said there would always be wars and rumors of war.[19] History has sadly proven him right. All around us wars wage—nation against nation, tribe against tribe, people against people, brother against brother. Human history is like a fire out of control. It seems that violence will always rage and that peace will always elude us. Yet Jesus was equally convinced that he knew the way to peace and that peace would in the end stand as victory.

For wars to end, there would have to be the end of violence.

For violence to cease, there would have to be the end of hatred and greed.

For hatred and greed to breathe their final breaths, forgiveness and generosity would have to take their places.

Where there is peace, there is no fear. Where there is fear, there is no peace. So then the journey for peace begins within our hearts. This is why we must face our fears, stand in our pain, and walk courageously into the uncertainty and mystery of a better future.

It may seem like a small thing, but when you get up in the morning and face your fears, you are participating in the redemption of the universe. When you refuse to allow yourself to be paralyzed by the uncertainty of tomorrow and set forth with courage and faith, you become part of creating a new world—a better world.

The peace that your soul longs for is the very peace the world needs. I cannot speak of peace and not speak of Jesus, for it is Jesus alone who leads us to the way of peace. The way of Jesus is the way of the warrior. It is Jesus who is the warrior of peace. There are not different kinds of peace, just different contexts where peace can be realized. When you have won the battle for inner peace, you now carry within you what the world desperately needs. It is only when you have inner peace that you can bring peace to a world at war with itself. The warrior fights for peace.

The Warrior Seeks to Become Invisible

The warrior does not need to be seen. They are most powerful when they are invisible. It is impossible to defeat an enemy you cannot see or disarm a warrior whose weapon never seems to strike. The warrior knows that lesser opponents depend on swords and bows and arrows, but the weapon of the warrior is their wisdom.

Wisdom is hard to define but easy to identify. It cannot be purchased or easily gained. You may overpower an enemy and yet still die a fool. While there are many expressions of wisdom, for our purposes it will be defined as the ability to bring peace. When the warrior is wise, they fight only for peace. The proof of their victory is that they have created a world where what is good and beautiful and true prevails. The fool is the enemy of wisdom. The fool is driven by greed and power and violence. The fool uses their weapons to harm, injure, and destroy. The warrior wields a weapon only to defend, protect, and liberate.

The warrior does not wield a weapon; they *are* a weapon. Their strength does not come from the weapons they hold but from the wisdom that has taken hold of them. The novice believes that their power lies in being seen; the warrior understands they are most powerful when they are unseen. The way of the warrior is not a path toward war but a path toward wisdom. The warrior knows they have not learned everything but that they know everything they need to learn.

Wisdom is the warrior's greatest weapon. When you have wisdom, you are never unarmed, you are never defenseless, and you are never powerless. You need skill to know how to shoot an arrow straight, but only wisdom can teach you how to never need to shoot it. Wisdom is not the result of having learned enough; it comes when you know there is never enough learning.

Wisdom is less like a deep ocean and more like the force of a river. The power of the river is in its ability to adapt to its environment, change its course when necessary, and yet always find its way toward its destiny. The river reminds us that it is not always the straight path that leads us to where we must go. The meandering of a river might cause you to think that it has lost its intention, yet the river, as wide as it may bend and as often as it may change its course, always moves forward toward its intended destination.

The warrior is like a river, with fluid and adaptive moves. The warrior is not rigid or unchanging. The warrior is not like a stone that cannot be broken but like water that even when cut in two cannot be divided. It is not a weapon that makes you a warrior—it is your wisdom.

Stealth Mode

My grandfather was a man who could be described as both a person of small stature and a man of great weight. I imagine this is the way they described Napoleon. He was one of those unusual people who, though he never grew taller than five foot five, had a presence that filled the room whenever he entered. It's hard to explain presence but easy to identify it. There are some people who seem to do nothing to garner our attention and yet the room tilts in their direction whenever they enter.

A man by the name of Hermanindo de Cardona was accustomed to carrying the weight of power and influence. In a nation where the poor get poorer and the rich get richer, he defied the odds and rose above the status of his birth, using his intellectual prowess to become a high-level government official in the nation of El Salvador. I will be forever indebted to him for shaping who I am. He taught me how to play chess when I was three years old, pulled out maps and explained to me continental drift when I was five, and taught me about global economics before I was ten.

One of the curious things about my grandfather was the way he would both stand and move when he was in a room. I remember he once told me never to lean against a wall because it was a sign of weakness but to always stand straight. I also remember when he was nearing a hundred years old how he refused to let me help him up and down stairs, insisting that he must do it for himself.

One of the funny things about my grandfather is that he always found it entertaining to move so silently that no one would realize he had entered the room. He loved being able to walk into a room, seemingly invisible to everyone who was there, and just stand there in his silence until someone realized he had been there all along. My grandfather taught me the power of being invisible, of not drawing too much attention to oneself, of conserving movement and cutting through sound.

The warrior understands that their greatest power is in what is not seen. Long before the warrior is seen or heard, they must be felt. The greatest of warriors wins battles without their opponent ever even knowing a war has been waged. Although others may see your skill with a bow or your expertise with a sword, you must never forget that your greatest weapon is wisdom.

Years ago I endeavored to describe the essence of wisdom in my book *Uprising*:

> An essential component of wisdom is the ability to get to the core. Wisdom always finds a way through the mess we make of life. It doesn't find the easiest way, but the way marked by the footprints of God. Wisdom knows that ancient paths will lead us into a divine future. Wisdom is the product of a sacred imagination. Wisdom knows the way to freedom. Where there is wisdom, there is always hope. Wisdom simplifies. Wisdom clarifies. Wisdom untangles. Wisdom unshackles. Wisdom illuminates. Wisdom liberates. In the end wisdom enlightens us to live lives of nobility.[20]

This is the highest expression of wisdom—to live our lives for others rather than ourselves. The fool lives to consume all they can take from the world. The wise live to create a better world. The way of the warrior is to choose the path of nobility. The warrior also understands that wisdom is gained not in a moment but in an endless number of moments in which choices must be made. The path toward wisdom is not taken by steps but by choices. When you choose to take, you choose the path of the fool. When you choose to give, you choose the way of the wise.

The warrior never fights out of anger; they fight only out of honor. They never fight to conquer; they fight only to liberate. The warrior fights against evil so that good may prevail. Wisdom is revealed by what a person fights for. If you fight for yourself, you have given yourself to too small a thing. The warrior fights against injustice, against poverty, against despair, against depression.

The wisdom of the warrior establishes both their enemies and their battles. Only the fool fights battles not worth fighting or even worth winning. Because of their wisdom, the warrior does not engage in battles that should not be fought. And at the same time, they do not shrink back from battles that must be fought. This is the true wisdom of the warrior. The warrior can win the battles where even the strongest have known only defeat. This is why the warrior is never powerless. You can try to take all their earthly weapons, but you cannot take their wisdom. And because the warrior has learned the way of wisdom, they are never powerless.

Invisible Leadership

Solomon was the wisest man who ever lived, and he once saw wisdom so great that it astonished even him. He wrote in his annals, known as Ecclesiastes,

> I also saw under the sun this example of wisdom that greatly
> impressed me: There was once a small city with only a few
> people in it. And a powerful king came against it,
> surrounded it and built huge siege works against it. Now
> there lived in that city a man poor but wise, and he saved the
> city by his wisdom. But nobody remembered that poor man.
> So I said, "Wisdom is better than strength." But the poor
> man's wisdom is despised, and his words are no longer
> heeded. The quiet words of the wise are more to be heeded
> than the shouts of a ruler of fools. Wisdom is better than
> weapons of war, but one sinner destroys much good.[21]

We are not given many details about this unknown man's life or of the circumstance in which Solomon discovered him. And it is curious that of all the different encounters in Solomon's life, he found this one to be the most noble expression of wisdom. I would assume he came to know many great kings and queens. He sat at the table and shared meals with the most powerful men and women of his time. He had available the greatest thinkers and the most profound philosophers and the most skilled artisans the world had

ever known. Why is it that here Solomon finds wisdom that aston-
ishes him?

Solomon is described as the wisest man who ever lived. But the
one thing he was never able to know was what his wisdom would
have looked like without his wealth and power and status. His wisdom would always be seen through the vantage point of his stature.
Solomon understood the power of wisdom when combined with
wealth and position and power. Here in this moment, he was able
to see the power of wisdom stripped of any advantage. Here Solomon saw the power of invisible leadership.

Scripture tells us, "There once was a small city with only a few
people in it," which means that it was a city very different from
Jerusalem. It was not an epicenter of power and influence; it was an
obscure city. In fact, it would be better described as a town. And in
that city there were only a few people. It was not a hustling me-
tropolis with endless activity and trade, but for some reason a great
king decided to conquer it. An ominous, powerful king suddenly
surrounded the small city, built a huge siege work around it so no
one could enter and no one could leave, and eventually conquered
the city and held it captive.

The details are left out, but the implications are clear. It is un-
likely that even this city fell without a fight. This had to be a moment filled with loss and grief, with hopelessness and despair. Those
young men who had trained all their lives to protect their city and
its citizens had failed in their efforts. Their blood filled the streets.
The weeping and wailing of widows and orphans must have created

a deafening sound across the city gates. Yet there lived in that city a man who was poor but wise. I am convinced this is what caught Solomon's eye. Solomon had never known what it meant to be poor. He always had access to every resource he could ever need or desire. But this man had nothing available to him—no wealth, no power, no status, no weapons, no army. Only wisdom was available to him, and he saved his city by his wisdom.

Can you imagine saving a city with nothing in your hand except the wisdom you've gained and stored in your heart? Solomon failed to give us the details of how this was done. Maybe he never knew how. Maybe he was incapable of seeing how it was possible, and he could see only the conditions and the outcome. What seemed to bother Solomon the most was that nobody remembered that poor man, which might explain why he remains unnamed. Solomon probably used all his resources to try to uncover the identity of this one poor wise man who set an entire city free but who was remembered by no one. It's almost as if he were invisible: no one saw him, no one heard him, but no one could deny what he had done.

From this, Solomon came to a profound conclusion that he could have never known from his own personal experience: wisdom is better than strength. What Solomon was not doing here is creating a dichotomy between wisdom and strength. Wisdom is not the opposite of strength, nor is wisdom the absence of strength. It might be fair to say that without wisdom, strength becomes a weakness. But what Solomon was discovering is that wisdom has its own power.

For nearly ten years of my life, I worked in one of the most violent districts in the United States. For years, my daily patterns put me near the world of drug cartels and some of the world's most violent people, yet never once did I carry a gun, or any weapon, for that matter. I could not possibly begin to count the number of times I would be in the middle of an intense encounter between the police and those suspected of criminal activity. There were numerous times when gang warfare was avoided simply because we chose to stand in between the two parties. All those moments needed in order to explode was one person to lose their cool and pull the trigger.

In each of those situations, the environment was already unstable, and violence was the norm. It would have been easy to rationalize that I needed to protect myself and carry a weapon too, yet the only reason I am alive and writing these words right now is that all my weapons were unseen. Even in the most volatile circumstances, I was convinced that wisdom could bring peace, even if just for a moment.

In a much less dramatic environment, I found this principle to be true as a husband and father. To stay married for thirty-five years takes more than love; it takes wisdom. No matter how much you love someone, you will inevitably have conflict and disagreements. Wisdom understands that it is less important to win a fight or a point than it is to win the person. Wisdom knows that you should never fight against people; you should fight for them. What's the point of winning a fight if you lose the person? When you love someone, the real fight is to keep winning that person.

This is the way of the warrior—not simply that wisdom is better than strength but that wisdom *is* our strength. To strike a sword as a fool is only to add to the violence. Wisdom never seeks to wound except to heal. Wisdom never longs for war but for peace.

You can almost feel the tension that was tearing at Solomon's soul. He heard about a poor man who set an entire city free by using only wisdom, while he was the son of King David, a man of war. In fact, the very reason Solomon was commissioned to build the temple was that his father had blood on his hands. All Solomon had ever known was a history of violence, but that violence was the very reason Solomon inherited a time of peace.

We might wonder why God would involve himself in the wars of men, yet the reality is that this is the only history we have. Human history is a history of war. God intervenes in a broken world and steps into our violence, knowing only he can bring us peace.

As Solomon looked more carefully at the aftereffect of the poor man's life, he realized that not only was the man forgotten but that after he secured his city's freedom, the people despised his wisdom and no longer wished to hear what he had to say. Solomon saw from this moment that wisdom is better than the weapons of war, though it was equally clear to him that wisdom brings no promise of fame, recognition, or even respect. The most dangerous thing in the world is to put weapons in the hands of fools, and the most powerful force in the world is the wisdom that makes us drop our weapons.

It is the quiet words of the wise that are more powerful than the shouting of a ruler of fools. We have come to confuse the ability to make noise with the power of having a voice. The fool feels powerful because they have a weapon in their hand; the warrior knows they are powerful when their hands are empty.

Though the way of the warrior is a way of peace, you will have many battles to fight. Each battle will require different skills and weaponry. The one weapon you must always take with you is wisdom. It is the one resource that is endless and without limit. If you take wisdom with you, you will always have everything you need. In that sense the wise are never impoverished. One of the perplexing things about wealth is that if you take on a big enough challenge, you will be overwhelmed by your sense of poverty. When you pursue a great mission, you will inevitably feel that you don't have enough resources for the task.

Wealth cannot secure your victory, and poverty cannot prevent it. There is no more powerful situation than to be poor with nothing but wisdom as you engage to save your city. A rich fool is not more powerful than a poor sage. Never let your lack of resources justify your lack of ambition. Never allow the measure of your wealth to be the measure of your life. Solomon was a man with both great wealth and great wisdom, but now he could see clearly that only great wisdom ensures the best future.

There was a time in our lives when Kim and I slept on the floor because we could not afford a bed, but this did not diminish our joy nor steal our intention. The scope of our dreams was not limited to the size of our income. In the same way, that lack of resources must not limit the battles you fight. You must not allow yourself to be paralyzed by what seem to be overwhelming circumstances. It's absurd for one poor man to think he could set an entire city free. What in the world was he thinking? Couldn't he see that those who were better prepared than he was, more skilled than he was, more talented than he was, more powerful than he was, had already failed in pursuit of the same outcome? Yet somehow he seemed undaunted in his determination to do what everyone else would certainly know was impossible.

History would tell us that one poor man could not set an entire city free. Precedent would reinforce that this would be a ridiculous endeavor. Yet while the warrior is informed by the past, they are not formed by it. The warrior is not formed by what has been done and what can't be done; the heart of the warrior is formed by what must be done.

I have lived long enough to see things come to pass that were once considered impossible. I have also lived long enough to know that the impossible never surrenders to the possible without a fight. The poor man in this story began with nothing. He was determined to set his entire city free, knowing that he must go to war against what Solomon described as a powerful king. The warrior knows that every great endeavor comes with great opposition.

I hope you will never have to know the violence of war. I hope you will never have to experience the devastation that countless millions have already come to know. I come from a nation with a history of violence. I was born in a city that bears the burden of having one of the highest murder rates in the world. The children of El

Salvador have never had the luxury of childhood. When other children were holding crayons, they were holding weapons.

My greatest hope would be that we would all come to know a day when there is no more war. That hope is why I write these words and call you to walk this path. This is the power of wisdom—to fight the battles that matter most so that we never have to fight another war again. If we study war, it is only to find our way to peace. Solomon described this poor man as having the greatest wisdom he had ever seen, not because he went to war, but because he found a way to peace.

There are some who fight meaningless battles against lesser opposition simply to confirm their own sense of greatness. Actually, one of the most common critiques of professional boxing is that even the best boxers, after having achieved the pinnacle of success, hold on to their titles not by maintaining their level of skill and strength but by being properly managed. Once you win the belt, the rest of your career is less about maintaining your level of greatness and more about avoiding the wrong fights and the wrong fighters. This is one of the reasons professional boxing careers often end so badly. Eventually the wrong opponent becomes unavoidable. Suddenly you find yourself in the ring with a hungry fighter who has no respect for your legend. He quickly proves you to be too slow, too old, and far past your prime.

The warrior never fights for themselves; they fight only for others. They never use what they do not have as an excuse, they never use the overwhelming nature of the challenge as an escape, and they are never surprised when faced with unexpected and undeserved opposition.

The enemy that we tend to expect is like the powerful king who came and seized the city. The enemies we rarely speak of are the ones within us—those that would cause us to live in fear and so paralyze us that we would rather live a life of oppression than pay the price for freedom. We would expect an enemy king and his soldiers to fight against our revolt. The stories that are rarely told are the ones of the very people we are trying to set free, people turned against us because we are endangering the status quo. I have come to know the painful truth in life: most people would rather live in the predictability of captivity than risk the uncertainty that comes in a fight for freedom.

It may seem completely counterintuitive, but in my experience, depressed people are the least likely to be willing to change any of their life patterns. In other words, people who hate their lives are the least likely to change them. When you love your life, you are more open to change. When you somehow find yourself in a life you never wanted, it has a paralyzing effect. It becomes a subtle version of Stockholm syndrome, where you develop an unhealthy relationship to your captor and disdain for anyone trying to set you free.

I've learned this lesson the hard way over the past forty years. I have tried one too many times to help people move out of lives they hate to lives they could love. The problem is that the change could not come without risk. I have seen this time and again. People will stay in jobs they hate for an unimaginable number of years. They will stay in destructive relationships because the fear of being alone feels overwhelming to them. If you are not living the life you long for and have the power to choose a different life, then what is keeping you from your freedom? Is there a siege work that has been built around your life that needs to be torn down? The wisdom of the warrior is your way to freedom.

The poor man's wisdom would not only have to overcome the military prowess of this conquering king but also have to set his people free from the crippling power of oppression and the fear that must have overtaken their hearts. When a people are conquered, they do not simply lose their land, homes, and freedom; they also lose their hopes and dreams and future. The poor man would have to overcome despair with hope and convince the people that there was a future worth fighting for. The first siege work that would have to be broken is the one that held them captive in fear. Before they would fight for freedom, they would have to choose to live free.

We see it only in the aftermath of this man's life, but the way of wisdom never seeks fame, even while living for greatness. This man was unknown before the story began and unremembered after the story was over. Clearly, if he knew how to set a city free, he also knew how to secure his own fame. It mattered to Solomon that he would be remembered throughout history. It mattered to Solomon that he would not be forgotten. For Solomon, fame was inseparable from greatness. But for this poor man who was wise, for this man who had set his entire city free, to be known seemed unimportant.

And we must ask ourselves, do we seek to be known more than to be worth knowing?

My grandfather could walk in and out of a room without being heard. The poor man walked in and out of history without being remembered. The greatest warrior cannot be heard when they strike, cannot be seen when they move. When all is said and done, the warrior is not known for their weapons but for their wisdom. And while the poor man was quickly forgotten, what he did was never forgotten. Solomon could not find his name, but his fingerprints were everywhere. The warrior lives their life to leave a legacy and live their legend.

When we are young, we are drawn by the fight far more than compelled by the training. We love the sound of victory far more than the grind of discipline. When you understand that wisdom is your greatest strength, you do not neglect the work necessary to sharpen your edge. It is Solomon who also reminds us that "if the ax is dull and its edge unsharpened, more strength is needed, but skill will bring success."[22] Too often we waste our strength by trying harder rather than becoming sharper.

There is a reason I love the story of the poor man who set his city free. The central figure of this story overcomes the very obstacles that all of us will face. Although his was an epic battle against a great empire, ours may be the ordinary battles of everyday life. Like this poor man, all of us will face our own struggle against a sense of insignificance. We must embrace the power of one person with God. At some point or another, we will feel as if we are underresourced for the challenges ahead. We must lean into the unlimited resources of the God who calls us. If not all of us, certainly most of us will wonder if we have the necessary position or power to accomplish our greatest challenges. It is then we must embrace the power of influence. In the end, most of us will wonder if what we've given ourselves to has been worth the fight, especially if no one remembers our names. And that's why we must never forget that what is done for ourselves will one day be forgotten but that what we have done for others will be remembered for eternity.

Keep Your Edge

Years ago I took my turn at being a lumberjack. In my twenties, when I had no idea what I wanted to do with my life, I tried an endless number of jobs, but most of them were just for the simple purpose of paying the bills. So as a lumberjack, I traveled with a crew to the mountains of Virginia to cut down giant trees in a section of the woods that needed to be cleared.

It was an ideal scenario. Because the government needed free labor to clear the land, we could sell the lumber and clear significant profits for our work. I've never liked being paid by the hour. I've always been drawn to opportunities where my income is not limited by my willingness to work harder than everyone else. When you are being paid not by the hour but by the pound, there is no time to waste.

When you are a novice, you cut away at the tree, never taking

the time to pull back and sharpen the ax's edge. Frankly, when you
are inexperienced, you don't even notice that the edge has become
dull. You do notice that the tree becomes denser and every inch of
progress becomes harder and harder. If you're not paying attention,
you'll simply think that you're losing strength or that in some
strange way the tree is gaining strength. It takes a more seasoned
lumberjack to make you aware that you are increasing your effort
but decreasing your result.

The fool just keeps striking and striking without paying attention to the quality of the edge. The wise know that if the edge is
unsharpened, more strength is needed. The warrior understands
that behind one strike of their sword are ten thousand hours in
which they have wielded their sword without an enemy present. It
is no different in life, that we are not pulling back bows or swinging
swords or carrying the weapons of conventional battle. Every life is
a series of battles, of conflicts, and of wars, and of course the war we
speak of is the one that rages within. You cannot win the battle for
your soul if you choose to live the life of a fool, neglecting the health
of your soul and not taking time to refine who you are.

The battle may look different for each of us, but the battle line
is the same: it is at the intersection of our passions and desires. Solomon tells us to love wisdom. He knows that in the end we become
what we love. We do not become fools because we lack the right
information; we become fools because we love the wrong things.
The only way you can care for your soul is to nurture your love for
what is good and beautiful and true.

Solomon also tells us that "the fear of the LORD is the beginning of wisdom."[23] Why is the fear of God the starting point on the path toward wisdom? To begin with, what you fear has mastery over your life. If you fear only God, then he becomes your only master. What you fear also establishes the boundaries of your freedom. If you are afraid of heights, you stay low. If you are afraid of crowds, you stay alone. Fear limits your freedom except when it comes to God.

Scripture tells us that "perfect love casts out fear."[24] When we fear God and God alone, our fear is consumed in his perfect love. It is only when we love him that his love casts out all our fear. So when we love the Lord our God with all our hearts and souls and strength and minds, fear no longer has power over our lives. We are finally and most beautifully free.

In summary, if you want to stop being a fool, stop loving the wrong things. (Have you ever noticed that fools always fall in love with the wrong people?) Second, realize that you were designed for God and that the health of your soul can come only by embracing his love for you. Third, recognize that the health of your soul is also an outgrowth of your love for God. Fourth, fuel the passion of your heart for all that is good and beautiful and true. And, finally, take the time necessary to nurture your desires and passions so that they reflect the heart of God himself.

Solomon's imagery, an unsharpened ax, is his way of reminding us that wisdom has the advantage of setting us up for success. The warrior spends their time refining their art, their craft, and their life.

While maintaining a posture of humility, there is a continuous pursuit of excellence. The warrior understands that every manifestation of greatness has hidden behind it a life of discipline, determination, and persistence. For the warrior, the beauty is in the details. As important as it is to watch the tree fall, it is important to see the edge sharpened. The ax matters to the warrior. The ax is not what you have but who you are. If wisdom is the weapon, then your character is the edge. You cannot fight the great battles that will come before you if you have not chosen to fight the battle within you.

Solomon's father once told him that "as iron sharpens iron, so one person sharpens another."[25] You cannot be made better than you are if you choose to live your life with those who would settle for less. If you are comfortable with where you are, you will never know how far you can go. If you refuse to change, then you refuse to grow.

Wisdom comes from the pain of critique and sometimes comes through the wounds of criticism. As when iron sharpens iron, wisdom comes only with friction and fire. The skills for life that Solomon speaks of come in the everyday decisions that will be mostly unnoticed—the choices we make that help us become the people we are, the choices that shape our character, the choices that create our future. Wisdom understands that choices have momentum. Wisdom understands that choices are our power.

You must never forget that there is no more spiritual act than to choose. Before you swing your ax, choose your tree. Decide what your life is about; decide what is worth living for; find your intention. And no matter what may come, no matter what battles ensue, never relinquish your intention. The fool swings mindlessly and chops once at every tree that stands in front of them. The warrior understands that not every battle is theirs, that not every tree is meant for them. When you take your ax, choose your tree and keep striking until that tree has fallen. When you move with wisdom, you know your strength. You see when certain choices make you dull and when other choices make you sharp.

There is nothing more debilitating than giving your strength to the wrong thing. When you live your life without intention, you make your edge dull. When you live a life of obligation, it steals from you your strength. Wisdom allows you to harness your strength. When you live your life with intention, you find your strength, and every time you strike the ax, you unexpectedly get stronger.

The warrior trains for the unexpected moment. They know that life is unpredictable, yet they are undaunted by this reality, for though they cannot plan what life will bring, they know they are prepared for it. They have sharpened their iron against the iron of others. They have taken the time to sharpen the edge of their ax.

There are certain markers you can look for to know you're chopping at the right tree. Some of them are more concrete, and some of them are more intuitive. One marker is who you are as a person. Your gifts and talents are at least a starting point for which battles are yours to fight or yours to walk away from. When you lack the natural gifting to do something, even when you care about it, you will always find yourself at a deficit. You have to look in a mirror and ask yourself the hard question, *Was I created to do this?*

A good follow-up question to ask yourself is, *Am I prepared to do this?* You may have the natural talent, but you haven't paid the price to develop the skills necessary to succeed. You may have the natural talent to be a neurosurgeon, but I don't want you in my head unless you've taken on the discipline of becoming a highly skilled medical professional. This may mean that it's the right tree but the wrong timing. There are battles you will fight later in life, but right now it's boot camp, and you're still in training.

Another marker to help you know if you are spending your strength in the right place is your passion and energy. If you are passionate about the process and not just the outcome, that's a marker that you are on the right track. If you are energized by the hard work and not simply its promise of success, that's a great marker that you are chopping at the right tree.

An external marker can be the impact that your actions have on others. You may get sick every time you are invited to be a public speaker, but the influence you have on the audience is undeniable. Oftentimes I have seen highly talented people who are terrified by the callings that are on their lives, and the only thing that keeps them swinging the ax is a sense of responsibility for the good that is being accomplished in the lives of others. This for me is one of the most altruistic and noble reasons to be motivated to create wealth. For some, their responsibility is not simply to have a job but to create jobs. It's not enough to simply gain wealth; they must create wealth so that the welfare of others is affected by their work. In the end, everything we do should ultimately be measured by how much good is done for others.

Although life may not have yet brought you wealth or position or power, there is no poverty that can stop you from fulfilling God's intention for your life when you are walking in wisdom. This is why it matters who you walk with as well. When you choose to live your life in concert with others who are willing to pay the high price of pursuing the greatest challenges and developing their full potential and capacity, it shapes who you are. Lean in to those who refuse to leave you the same. Stay close to those who see you as more than you are in this present moment. Never forget that the rebuke of a friend is of greater value than the kiss of an enemy.[26]

Wisdom knows that the way of the warrior cannot be walked alone. And while you may find yourself at some point to be a solitary source of hope needed to bring an entire city freedom, the wise know that wisdom was never gained alone. They also know that we were never meant to do life alone.

Solomon reminds us, "Two are better than one, because they have a good return for their labor: If either of them falls down, one can help the other up. But pity anyone who falls and has no one to help them up. Also, if two lie down together, they will keep warm. But how can one keep warm alone? Though one may be overpowered, two can defend themselves. A cord of three strands is not quickly broken."[27]

It's somewhat ironic that these words from Solomon are almost exclusively quoted at weddings, when the actual context for saying these words has nothing to do with marriage. The context is actually about a man who has gained immeasurable wealth but finds himself without either a son or brother. He comes to the end of his life and realizes that his wealth is of no value because he has lived his life alone, disconnected from others. Life, Solomon reminds us, is filled with unexpected twists and turns. And with all we do not know about the future, what we can be certain of is that there will be struggles, challenges, and battles ahead. Life is a great quest, but even the hero knows it should not be faced alone.

While the warrior is invisible, they know that in the eyes of those that matter, they are fully seen. Fame's great illusion is that you are known by the masses.

Fame's great danger is to be known by no one. The warrior does not need a crowd; they need a tribe. Though the warrior seeks to be invisible, they know that in the eyes of those that matter, they are fully seen. The warrior knows that wisdom gives them the power of invisibility.

CODE 3

The Warrior Finds
Honor in Service

The warrior lives in the paradox between service and greatness. The warrior is always first a servant. Contrary to popular perception, a life of service does not diminish the pursuit of greatness. The warrior must learn to walk with both humility and ambition. The warrior does not serve because they cannot lead; they know that a person cannot lead if they do not serve. Every day for the warrior is a pursuit of excellence. In the warrior there can be no hint of apathy or complacency. The warrior has too much honor to give anything less than their very best to their master. Every day is a competition against who they were yesterday.

The warrior is indifferent to fame while at the same time is relentlessly pursuing greatness. They see fame as what you do for yourself and greatness as what you do for others. Greatness is not the absence of humility; it is the absence of apathy. Just as you can be famous and not be great, you can be great and not famous.

Although the warrior may gain great fame, it is never their ambition. Let fame be the food of lesser men.

The warrior pursues their legend. The warrior pursues the life they must live, the battle they must fight, the sacrifice they must make. To the warrior, greatness is not the product of ego but of service. If you live for yourself, you can settle for less. If you live for others, it requires all of who you are. This is why the warrior never envies the greatness of others but in fact honors and admires it. The life of the warrior is defined by the pursuit of greatness. This is their greatest act of service.

There is a young man at Mosaic, our church here in Los Angeles, whom I have known almost all his life. I have worked with his father and have watched him grow into an extraordinary individual. Even as a young boy, he would come to ask me questions that would always amaze me. His inquiries were deep, thoughtful, and even provocative. So I was not surprised when he came to me again, now as a man, asking one more profound question. I expected it to be about the meaning of life or the nature of our existence. However, the question he chose to ask *did* catch me by surprise: "Is it wrong to be competitive?"

Honestly, this question really threw me off, as I didn't think that anyone at Mosaic would have to ask this question. But I understand why this was a struggle for him. Shane is extremely competitive. In fact, by his own description, he loves assessing the room, figuring out who is the best, and then determining how to outdo that person. What I thought was interesting was that I had, in more than twenty years of teaching, never even implied that it was wrong to be competitive. Where did this tension come from for him?

The reality is that we live in a time in history in which competition is seen as something that needs to be eliminated. Our schools are not only eliminating the designation of winners and losers, but they have actually gone as far as to eliminate scoring altogether so no one knows who is ahead and who is behind.

We are far more comfortable with the language of cooperation and collaboration than we are with the language of competition. Our negative view of competition is often put on hold when we watch such events as the Olympics, the World Cup, the Super Bowl, and the NBA Finals. But as a whole, we have adopted a framework that suggests that competition is archaic and antiquated and must be eliminated from the human story. Yet without competition, we lack the necessary context to push ourselves beyond our own capacities.

Competition, when understood properly, makes you better, makes you more, makes you stronger. My response to Shane was that it is not wrong to be competitive, an answer he wasn't expecting to hear.

He said, "So is it okay for me to look around the room and compare myself to others?"

I responded to him, "I thought you wanted to be the best?"

A little bit insulted, he responded immediately, "I do want to be the best."

I said, "Well, when you are the best, there is no one to compare yourself to. So rather than comparing yourself to others, why don't you compete against you, who you are today. That way when you are the best, you're still competing against the same person: who you were yesterday."

Roger Bannister was the first person to break the four-minute mile. He didn't have to break the four-minute mile to be the best in comparison to others. In fact, no one in the world ever expected him to break the four-minute mile. That barrier was perceived as impossible to cross. If he had measured what it meant to be best against others, he never would have accomplished the "impossible."

When you're the best, you don't compare yourself against others; you compare yourself against the impossible. After Bannister broke the four-minute mile, it changed the standard for every athlete that followed him. He changed the meaning of what it meant to be the best, and, ironically, his accomplishment made everyone in his field better. Today, breaking a four-minute mile is routinely done by world-class athletes.

I think part of the unease we feel about the idea of being competitive, especially for followers of Jesus, is that we also want to be people of humility and reflect the character of Christ. I'm convinced that a great part of our discomfort with the language of pursuing greatness centers around Jesus's conversations with his disciples. On one occasion Jesus and his disciples were traveling to Capernaum. When they had arrived and were resting in a house, Jesus asked the others what they had been arguing about on the road. They kept quiet and did not want to disclose to him that their conversation had focused on who was the greatest.[28]

I don't have to eavesdrop on that conversation to know what they didn't say. I know they didn't say that Jesus was the greatest. After all, if the Twelve were talking about who was the greatest and their immediate response was "Jesus," they would have eagerly revealed to him what they had been talking about when he asked.

It's kind of strange, if you think about it, that they were traveling with Jesus and when they began talking about who was the greatest, Jesus himself did not immediately come to mind. It would be like me and my team at Mosaic arguing about who is the best three-point shooter and walking with Steph Curry and not even mentioning him. Or what if you and a group of your friends were with Albert Einstein and you asked, "Who is the best at math?" It would be strange if "Einstein" wasn't everyone's immediate response.

How is it possible that Jesus's twelve disciples would throw out any options other than him as being the greatest among them? But they hadn't, and that's exactly why they stayed quiet. It shouldn't surprise us that a natural conversation about greatness emerged. The disciples were walking with greatness. If you were traveling with Mozart, you would inevitably talk about music. If you were traveling with Picasso, you would most certainly begin talking about art. Jesus, though, didn't inspire a conversation about a particular application of greatness but about the essence of greatness itself. The disciples were not asking who was the greatest at a particular feat; they were asking who was the greatest in the eyes of God.

This is a question only Jesus could inspire. His greatness was not the outcome of his talent or a particular ability; his greatness was about the totality of who he was as a person. Jesus epitomized what it meant to be human. He was the sum total of everything the disciples aspired to be. One of the particularly beautiful things about true greatness is that it leaves no room for envy. Jesus did not come to diminish the greatness in others; he came to awaken it. Even when he confronted the disciples about their conversation and their desire to take the seat of honor, he did not tell them to stop aspiring to be great; he simply redirected them so that they might succeed in their pursuit of greatness.

Keeping First Things Last

Then Jesus confounded them with words that have become well known across the world: "Anyone who wants to be first must be the very last, and the servant of all."[29] I am convinced that these words of Jesus have been terribly misunderstood. They have been heard over and over again as an admonition against the desire to be first. But in actuality he never discouraged the disciples from wanting to be first; he just told them what first looks like in his economy: *If you want to be first, then you must be last. If you want to be first, you must become the servant of all.* He didn't try to diminish their ambition; he tried to redirect their intention. Jesus wasn't trying to replace greatness with servanthood; he was trying to give us a new definition of greatness, which is servanthood.

On another occasion, the mother of John and James came to Jesus and asked him for a favor. He knew she had come with a question and asked her what she wanted as she was kneeling down in front of him, ready to make her petition on her sons' behalf. Her request was not for herself but rather for her two sons. She hoped they would sit at the right and left hands of Jesus in his kingdom.[30]

I don't know if you have a mom like that, but for me this would be an incredibly embarrassing moment. John and James were known as the "sons of thunder."[31] These two were rough-and-tough manly men, but they had their mom go on their behalf to ask for positions of honor that they did not deserve. It would be bad enough if your mother went to ask of Jesus something like this without letting you know, but what we discover is that her two sons were standing right behind her. I can't even imagine walking into the room behind my mom so she could ask on my behalf for the highest honors Jesus could give.

Jesus's response had a bit of a comedic element to it. He didn't answer her. He looked right at them and said, "You don't know what you are asking."[32] He forced them to step up and speak for themselves, and then the other disciples realized what was happening and became indignant with the two brothers. In my experience we become indignant when someone else asks for what we wanted.

So Jesus called them all together. At first he pointed to the examples that had influenced their perception of greatness. He said, "You know that the rulers of the Gentiles lord it over them, and their high officials exercise authority over them. Not so with you."[33] Jesus wanted them to know that the most common examples of greatness in their day were being wrongly measured. Rather, he suggested, "Instead, whoever wants to be become great among you must be your servant."[34]

Jesus's words are so powerful and so well known that we often miss the significance of his entire statement. No one had ever called their leaders to serve. All of the disciples saw the greatness in Jesus and assumed that his posture of servanthood was a short-term strategy. Yet this call to servanthood is not for everyone. It's actually very specific: it's a callout to whoever wants to become great. The call to servanthood finds its power only when it is received by those who are on the pursuit of greatness.

It is not wrong to aspire to greatness. The warning here is to be careful to never confuse fame with greatness. Otherwise, you may be aspiring to what is not really greatness at all. Fame is what you do for yourself; greatness is what you do for others. Jesus has unveiled to us how greatness is achieved in his kingdom. To be great, you must serve. So don't give up on your ambition to be great; instead, change your definition of what it means to be great and how greatness is achieved.

Most important, though, we need to change the why behind our drive. The question is not whether we should be competitive; the question is not whether we should pursue excellence; the question is not whether we should pursue greatness. The question is *why* we are pursuing it.

Paul told us, "Whether you eat or drink or whatever you do, do it all for the glory of God."[35] If you are to do all things for the glory of God, then there is nothing you should do where you are not aspiring to do your best, be your best, and, yes, even be *the* best. It is in service that your greatness will be found.

Jesus pressed further and once again reminded them, with even harsher language, that "whoever wants to be first must be your slave."[36]

Then he said, as the ultimate example of this paradox, "Just as the Son of Man did not come to be served, but to serve, and to give his life as a ransom for many."[37]

Jesus is not only the greatest man who ever lived but also the greatest servant who has ever lived. No one has ever served like Jesus, who gave his life as a ransom for us all, and no one will ever achieve his standard of greatness. Yet we too can be great if we will choose to serve and walk in the way of Jesus.

Unwrapping Power

It has always fascinated me that the words *samurai* and *deacon* have the same core meaning. They both mean "servant." The samurai were known as the greatest of warriors, yet they did not live for themselves. Their highest honor was to live lives of service for the one who was their lord.

Too often we have confused humility with powerlessness. Humility cannot be achieved from a posture of powerlessness. As long as we see ourselves as victims, humility does not come from a position of strength. True humility can be experienced only when we have come to know our power and use it for the good of others and not for ourselves.

When Jesus was asked which was the greatest of all the commandments, he responded that we are to love the Lord our God with all our hearts, souls, minds, and strength.[38]

We rarely focus on the last aspect of that commandment, to love God with all our strength. God assumes we have strength and that it will be used only for his ultimate good when that strength is fueled by God's love.

Maybe a good exercise would be to sit down and make a list of all your strengths. After all, you can't take mastery over what you are unaware of. Your intellectual capacity is a strength. Your physical health is a strength. Your emotional intelligence is a strength. Your ability to influence is a strength. Your ability to create wealth is a strength. Your resilience and determination are strengths. And the list can go on and on and on.

You need to know your power, and you need to take ownership of it, not to mention the power that has been placed within you because of the presence of God's Spirit in your life. If the God who created the entire universe dwells in your heart, how could you ever consider yourself powerless?

When Jesus walked among us, he emptied himself of all power and made himself to be nothing. He emptied himself of those divine attributes we admire the most. When God took on flesh and blood and entered this world as an infant, he relinquished the power that was rightfully his. In fact, Jesus once explained, "Apart from the Father I can do nothing."[39]

One evening Jesus gathered his disciples to eat together. At that time, he knew that Judas was already prepared to betray him.[40] John tells us that on this night there was a significant shift in the journey of Jesus of Nazareth. He came into this world having emptied himself of all his divine power, but now "Jesus knew that the Father had put all things under his power, and that he had come from God and was returning to God."[41]

What would you do the moment you knew that God the Father had put all things under your power? What would you do with unlimited power? What would your very first demonstration of your power be?

This is what makes Jesus different than the rest of us. After Jesus knew he had all things under his power, he got up from the meal, took off his outer clothing, and wrapped a towel around his waist. Then he poured water into a basin and began to wash his disciples' feet, drying them with a towel that was wrapped around him.[42]

I daresay, no master has ever chosen to serve his disciples like this. It seemed that nothing was beneath Jesus, no act of service too low or common. Peter was of course taken aback by Jesus's attempt to wash his feet and did everything he could to refuse his kindness. Yet Jesus insisted, "Unless I wash you, you have no part with me."[43]

How strange that this would be the way of God: "Unless I wash you, unless you let me serve you, unless you allow me to do this that is beneath me, you will never know the full measure of my love for you." We understand that Jesus came to save the world. I think it's harder for us to accept that he came to *serve* the world. He is the Savior of all because he is the servant of all. This is the way of the warrior: to serve is to sacrifice. To serve is to give oneself for the good of others. Jesus used his power to serve, and in this moment of servanthood, we see his greatness.

Choosing the Front Line

Perhaps the most memorable moment in the life of David occurred when he, as a young man, offered to go to war against Goliath. Goliath was, of course, the giant who taunted both God and the armies of Israel, knowing there was not one warrior in all Israel with the courage to fight him. David was at the battlefield that day only to deliver cheese. He was an errand boy. No one thought of him as a warrior. When the people looked at David, they saw only a servant. When David offered his services to King Saul, the man tried to dissuade David, telling him, "You are not able to go out against this Philistine and fight him; you are only a young man, and he has been a warrior from his youth."[44]

David responded to King Saul, "Your servant has been keeping his father's sheep."[45]

David's understanding of himself was that he was nothing more than a servant. But listen as he describes what it means to be a faithful servant: "When a lion or a bear came and carried off a sheep from the flock, I went after it, struck it and rescued the sheep from its mouth. When it turned on me, I seized it by its hair, struck it and killed it."[46]

Now, that sounds like a warrior to me, but David seemed to be pretty sure this was just a normal part of being a servant. He explained further, "Your servant has killed both the lion and the bear; this uncircumcised Philistine will be like one of them, because he has defied the armies of the living God. The LORD who rescued me from the paw of the lion and the paw of the bear will rescue me from the hand of this Philistine."[47]

David had one posture: servanthood. Because he saw himself as a servant, he was a shepherd like no one had ever known. I feel pretty safe in suggesting that it would've been a rare thing for a shepherd to go after a lion or a bear just to rescue a sheep. I imagine that if most shepherds saw a lion carrying off one of their sheep, they would've considered it the cost of doing business. They probably would just accept the fact that they were going to lose some sheep. These were not even David's sheep; they were his father's. Why on earth would he risk his own life to save one sheep that wasn't even his own property?

David understood the way of the warrior. He understood that to serve is the highest honor and that if you are a shepherd, you must aspire to be the greatest shepherd that has ever tended sheep. So he pursued the lion and he pursued the bear, and when they turned on him, he seized them by the hair and struck them and killed them.[48] David made being a shepherd look a lot like being a warrior. As a shepherd, he learned the skills that made him a warrior. David redefined what it meant to be a shepherd. Soon he would redefine what it meant to be a warrior.

His first battle as a warrior was against a giant. Instead of taking the armor that warriors always wore, he redefined both what a warrior fights with and how a warrior fights. No one had ever gone to battle with just five smooth stones. No warrior had ever gone against a giant with nothing more than a slingshot. No warrior had left behind their armor, leaving themselves completely exposed. No warrior had chosen agility above protection.

In the years to come, David would become known across the land as the greatest warrior of his time, yet even as a warrior, David redefined the standards of being a man of war. We need to remember that when David fought Goliath, he was still a shepherd. For him, fighting the giant was like fighting the bear or the lion. He wasn't fighting for his own glory or his own fame; he was fighting because no one else would and because he understood what was at stake. When he killed the lion and the bear, there was no audience and no applause. God and God alone knew David's actions and knew his heart.

The shepherd boy courageously confronted an enemy that all the warriors feared facing. It was David the servant who redefined what it meant to be a shepherd. It was David the shepherd who redefined what it meant to be a warrior. And it was David the warrior who would redefine what it meant to be a king. David killed Goliath not for himself but to defend the honor of God and the freedom of his people. This act of heroism should have forever indebted Saul to David, but we soon discover that Saul became filled with envy over David's growing fame.

After a time, King Saul turned against David. The very king whom David had fought for and protected now wanted him dead. David knew that Saul had attempted to assassinate him multiple times and that he was alive simply because the king was unsuccessful. Yet when David had an opportunity to kill King Saul, when he had the support of his men if he had chosen to do so, he established a standard of honor that no one had ever expected. He declared that he would not touch God's anointed one and that as long as Saul was king, David would not harm him. What we can see without question is that while David was still a warrior, he was already acting like a king.

You might look at David's life and think there were three different postures. The first, David the shepherd, then David the warrior, then David the king. But David had one role: David the servant. David the servant who served as a shepherd, David the servant who served as a warrior, David the servant who served as king. Servanthood is not a stage of life; it is a posture of the heart.

There is one other dynamic to this process that should not be overlooked. It is not only true that the warrior is called to serve; it is also equally true that the servant must become a warrior. David was a warrior both when he was a shepherd and when he became a king. As a shepherd, he fought to protect his sheep. As a king, he fought to protect his people. The spirit of a servant is to sacrifice one's own life for the good of those they serve.

Still, David reminds us that there is a difference between the way of the warrior and becoming a man of war. The way of the warrior is always a posture of servanthood. Our strength was never meant to be an act of violence or aggression, yet in David we see glimpses of our most heroic selves. He saved a sheep from the mouth of a lion; he killed Goliath with the swing of a stone; he established a nation; he called the people to love God and serve him only.

By any measure, David was a great man. And as we will discover by any measure, he was painfully flawed. This should not discourage us but rather give us hope. We are told that David was a man after God's own heart. The heart of God is the heart of a servant. This is the heart that David struggled to have formed in himself.

Hidden Ambition

When I was talking to Shane, the young man from church, I immediately began to think of the surgeon who saved my life when I was fighting cancer. In more than six hours of surgery, Dr. Khalili carefully and skillfully removed each cancer cell while protecting every healthy organ, assuring me the highest quality of life after the surgery was done. I told Shane, "I have a theory. I think Dr. Khalili is very competitive. I think he hates to lose." I don't mean he is competitive against other surgeons; I mean he is competitive against death, against cancer, against losing a patient.

Now, you have to understand that Dr. Khalili is a fascinating individual: kind, compassionate, thoughtful, yet stoic. He would be the perfect poker player, as you just cannot read his face. He doesn't show you any unexpected emotions. He is very reserved and under control. This, by the way, is exactly how I want my surgeon to be.

A part of the follow-up after beating cancer is continuing a battery of tests for up to two years until you're given a clean bill of health. So I knew I would see Dr. Khalili again. After my next visit and hearing the good news that I was cancer free, I decided to see if he would allow me to ask him a personal question. While we were standing in the hallway right before I was about to leave, I paused and said, "Dr. Khalili, I have a question I want to ask you."

He very graciously responded, "What is that?"

I said, "I was talking to this young man named Shane who was asking me if it is wrong to be competitive, and I told him about you. I told him I have a theory about you. I think that you are very competitive. In fact, I told him that I think you're so competitive that you hate to lose and that when you lose, you have trouble sleeping at night because it bothers you so much."

Then I paused to see what kind of response my thought solicited. At first there was nothing; he just looked at me with those very calm and stoic eyes, and for a second I thought I might be completely wrong. Then I saw it. The muscles on his face gave way to a deeper emotion. He began to smile—not just with his mouth but also with his eyes, almost as if he had reverted to being ten years old and had been found out about a secret he had kept so well. He responded, "I am so competitive. I am so competitive and I hate to lose."

It was a beautiful moment. I looked at him and I said, "Thank you for being competitive. Thank you for fighting against cancer. Thank you for refusing to lose me." I can't even imagine having a surgeon who wasn't competitive, who was okay with losing more patients than they saved. I certainly would never want a surgeon who was not driven to pursue greatness. Whoever holds the tools that cut into my body needs to have embraced the disciplines of deliberate practice and personal sacrifice.

Greatness is never found; it is gained. Greatness never comes easy; it's always the outcome of great discipline and hard work. If you're comfortable with where you are, if you're complacent, you will never discover the greatness that lies within. Complacency is like pouring water on coals. It is so important not to misunderstand the words of Jesus. Remember, he never said, "Don't be great." In fact, his invitation was for only those who aspire to greatness: "Whoever wants to become great among you must be your servant."[49] You will never know the power of servanthood until you know the fire of greatness.

Let no one tell you that ambition is not a virtue. Yes, Paul says, "Do nothing out of selfish ambition or vain conceit. Rather, in humility value others above yourselves, not looking to your own interests but each of you to the interests of the others."[50] But this is the key: it's in humility that we place others above ourselves. This must be our ambition.

The truth is, few of us see ambition as a virtue. We quietly think it's okay to be ambitious, but not too ambitious—too much ambition will corrupt us. But we never think that way about love. We never think, *Be careful not to love too much; you need to hold on to a little bit of hate.* We never think about forgiveness, *Be careful to not forgive too much; you need to hold on to a little bitterness.* Or about integrity, *Be careful not to have too much integrity; you need to keep a little bit of corruption.* But we understand virtues like love and forgiveness and integrity to be of such intrinsic value that one can't possibly pursue them too much.

The warrior understands that ambition is a virtue equal to compassion or kindness or even humility. We are to do nothing out of selfish ambition or vain conceit, but without ambition, we will find ourselves doing nothing and calling it humility. What we must do is bring the two universes of ambition and humility together since they were never intended to exist separately. We have a universe of thought around the concept of servanthood. When we think of servanthood, we attach words such as *humility, compassion, sacrifice,* and *selflessness.* These are the qualities by which we most readily understand Jesus to be defined.

The other universe consists of words related to ego and arrogance, and attached to that narrative are words such as *pride, selfishness, ambition, competition,* and even *greatness.* These, of course, would be understood as being contrary to the way of Jesus. The warrior understands these worlds must be brought together. Ambition, competition, and greatness can, and in fact must, exist in the same universe as humility, selflessness, and servanthood. Greatness cannot be achieved without sacrifice, and true servanthood is not the outcome of subservience but of passion.

You can choose both humility and ambition.

You can choose both competitiveness and selflessness.

You can choose both greatness and servanthood.

The truth that Jesus is trying to drive us to is that when these are brought together, we see ourselves best and most fully. In Buddhism, the ultimate end is the elimination of all desire. In the way of Jesus, our highest expression of being human is a life consumed with passion.

Play to Win

Even after all these years, I still love playing basketball. I played once with men my age, and I don't think I'll ever do it again. They were so old, so fragile, so slow. It was disturbing to realize they were my peers. I love playing against young men. It keeps me young, and most days, I have the pleasure of winning more than I lose. But on one particular day, I lost every single game. We had an odd number of players, and that meant that when I lost I had to sit. So I was doing a lot of losing and sitting that day. After about an hour of repeated and relentless humiliation, I went and sat down in a hallway to gather my thoughts and ask God why he was no longer with me.

A short time went by, when my son, Aaron, walked down this hallway, and as he passed me he said, "Pouting?" That did not sit well in my soul. When he came back the other way after going to the locker room, he said, "Still sitting here? Looks like you're pouting." I love my son, but he was really irritating in that moment.

I responded, "I'm not pouting. I'm just gathering my thoughts, getting myself ready to play again."

As he walked back on the court, since he had won again, he shouted back, "Still looks like you're pouting." So I got up, walked to the other court, grabbed a basketball, and began shooting to try to regain my stroke. As I stood there shooting by myself, I was totally unaware how much time had passed. The game on the other side of the court had ended, and my son walked over and said, "Hey, are you okay?"

I said, "Yeah, I'm okay."

"It doesn't seem like you're okay."

"I'm fine, Aaron. Stop asking me."

He said, "Well, Dad, it's your game, and you don't seem okay."

I said, "Son, I know I have hidden this well all your life, but I am really competitive, and I hate to lose." I'll never forget that moment. I was being so transparent. I was allowing my son to see the darkness of my own soul.

And he responded without hesitation, "Dad, you never hid it well. Everyone knows you're competitive, and everyone knows you hate to lose."

Then the thought hit me: I'd spent nearly sixty years trying to hide how competitive I was, and it didn't work anyway, so why didn't I just own it? I am competitive. I want to be the best. I want to pursue excellence every day of my life. I want to pay the price that greatness demands of me. I couldn't care less about fame, but I will live my life for greatness, and Jesus tells me how: by being the servant of all. This is the way of the warrior. The warrior is a servant, and that is their greatness.

So how will this play out in your own life? What is your field of play? Where have you been called to serve and aspire to greatness?

My journey as a communicator began among the urban poor.

Every week I would preach to small crowds, whether at the homeless shelter during the week or in the small house we would turn into a church every Sunday morning. The room was full of the poorest of the poor. Each seat was filled by former drug addicts or prostitutes or those struggling with an endless number of addictions. And when I say full, there were never more than forty or fifty people crammed into that house that we called church.

I remember praying even then, "God, these people never have the best of anything. Could you help me give them the very best on Sundays?" I aspired to be a great communicator not because I ever imagined myself preaching to large crowds or dared to believe anyone would ever read a book with my name on it, but because I just felt that those people deserved the best, and that drove me to aspire to be the best.

I don't know what your calling is. You may be a teacher or an architect or a doctor or a carpenter. But if you choose the way of the warrior, living a life of service, it will demand of you the best you have. You may not need to be great, but the world needs your greatness. Whatever God has placed within you that could ever be described as great was never meant for you, anyway. It's a stewardship that has been given to you. Greatness never belongs to the one who carries it; it belongs to the world that needs it.

Just think how your life would look if you decided greatness was your standard of your life as a parent, as a spouse, or as an employer or employee. For too long we have allowed apathy to masquerade itself as humility. There is nothing humble about living apathetic lives. In the same way, we cannot live lives of passion without unlocking our greatness.

Passion is the fuel of greatness, and love is the fuel of passion. When we love someone or something, we give them all of us. This is the elegant interconnection between servanthood and greatness. It is love that drives us to serve and love that drives us to greatness. This is why the two cannot be mutually exclusive. In the end, the one who serves is the one who is great, as they are the one who loves most profoundly.

The Warrior Frees Their Mind

The warrior cannot know their enemy if they do not know themselves. For the thousands of battles a warrior will face, their greatest battle comes when they truly see themselves. There is no territory more critical or difficult for you to take than that of your inner world. Your mind is also your minefield. To find the freedom to win your ultimate battle, you must fight to free your mind. Every battle that you will ever face in the outside world must first be won in your inner world.

This is why the warrior understands that they must know themselves, that they must know their mind. Though you may never live in a world defined by peace and beauty, the warrior has already come to know this world. You will never find a world that you cannot see. You cannot create a world that you do not know. You can bring to the world only what you have already fought for.

Your mind tells you what you will find. If your mind is set, you have limited what you will discover. If your mind is free, the possibilities are limitless. An open mind allows you to see opportunities that remain closed to those with limited thinking. An open mind opens the world to you. An open mind opens the future for you. It is only with an open mind that you are truly free to dream, to imagine, to create.

The mind is not separate from the heart. They are intertwined and inseparable. Two plus two equals four is only a concept until we have experienced it. Once we understand addition and then multiplication, we begin to see the power of limitless possibilities. Soon we experience that four minus two equals two. We begin to understand the power and even the pain of loss. We begin to know what it means to have and then to lose. Even simple math is wrapped in human experience.

In the same way, music is both mathematical and romantic. Every note carries within it emotion. Without a word being spoken, music speaks to the deepest part of the soul. There is no thought that is disconnected from emotion.

For the sake of imagery, I will speak of the heart as what carries all our experience and emotion, and the mind as the world that we create in response to the world around us as it intersects with the world within us. We do not see the world as it is; we see the world as we are.

A heart filled with violence will never see a world filled with peace. You can bring hope only if you have found hope. The mind can either blind you to the possibilities or give you sight to see what no one thought was ever possible. If you do not know your mind, you may very well be a prisoner of your limited thinking. When you know your mind, you are able to open your mind.

Have you ever noticed what it is that we remember—the memories that shape our lives and experiences that we never forget? In our minds, what we are trying to remember are our lives, but most of our lives have been forgotten. I can understand someone else forgetting my life. After all, most of my life is pretty much forgettable. Don't you find it strange that among all the people who have forgotten your life, you are one of them?

It's a peculiar realization to know that you have forgotten most of your life. Most of the experiences, the moments, the details— they all disappear, hidden behind selected memories that we call our past. But for every moment we remember, there must be at least a thousand others that we have forgotten. And we don't forget consciously; it happens without us even taking notice. We just forget to remember, and that is much easier than remembering to forget.

Some memories stick with us all our lives. They stick to us like peanut butter on the roof of our mouth: they are uncomfortable, even unwanted, and nevertheless our only choice is to swallow. Our memories create a maze through which our future experiences have to travel. The memories we remember create the barriers that we know. The memories we do not remember create the barriers that remain unknown. All of us have both visible and invisible barriers that we filter all our experiences through.

You must never forget to remember. When you know your mind, you know your memories—you choose your memories.

What you remember is how you shape your mind. Your memories are your mind's design. The root of the word *memory* is simply *mindful*.[51] Remembering is not a passive act; remembering demands of you perhaps your greatest mastery. You must take mastery over your memories. It is then and only then that you become mindful.

This is the beginning of knowing your mind. You can move the walls that have trapped you in limited thinking by changing what you choose to remember. If you find yourself confounded because everything you remember is negative, limiting, and destructive, there is only one path forward: you must create new memories.

The Space Between the Rain

When I was around ten years old, I began a reading binge. For whatever reason, reading became a great escape for me. Behind the doors of libraries, those ancient places where books were stored away, were the endless treasures of lives I'd never lived and words I'd never known. I remember reading an endless number of books, but most of the lines that once captured my attention have long left my memory.

So I have to think that it is not incidental that there is one line from one book that I have never forgotten. I don't remember the book, I don't remember its name, and I'm not sure who the author was, but I'll never forget the line. In the middle of an obscure story, the writer described a man who suffered from a particular malady. This may not be an exact quote, but it's exactly how I remember it:

"There was once a man who was driven to madness not because he could count the drops of rain but because he could count the spaces in between the drops of rain."

I imagine thousands upon thousands of people have read that same book and have passed by the same line, yet I have never met anyone who remembers it, so I always found it curious that I could not forget it. Having now lived five decades, it has become clear to me why of all the things I have forgotten, I never forgot this. These words strangely created in me a sense of hope—not that someone would be driven to madness because of the spaces between the rain but that someone out there actually understood the madness that raged within me. What for others may have seemed an absurd and poetic description of an unrealistic struggle was for me a diagnosis for which I did not have language to explain. How do you put into words the madness that comes from seeing every drop of rain and every space in between? The writer didn't offer me any solutions, but the cure strangely found me in the description.

For as long as I can remember, I have always suffered from a particular condition that I could not fully understand or describe. The best way to describe it is encompassed in the word *overload*. One aspect of it seemed to be external and the other internal, but it felt as though both aspects were driving me to madness.

Whenever I would walk into a room filled with people, I would feel as if I were being bombarded by unwanted information. It felt as if every detail in the room was crashing in my brain and demanding its attention. I seemed to lack the natural filters that allow most people to ignore much of what was happening around them. I felt as if I could see everything, and while that may sound like a super-power, it was absolutely debilitating. It would drive me to want to be alone so I could slow down the amount of data going into my head.

It was in 2013 that I went through a process in which I received some interesting information on my neurological patterns. I did receive some good news: I had an extraordinarily high level of impulse control and a significantly high level of focus. But where I had a deficit, it was extreme. I was in the bottom percentile of what was called NeuroSpeed, which makes me sound really slow.

I remember a conversation with one particular doctor. He explained that the best way to understand this phenomenon was with the imagery of shutter speed. Most people's brains have rapid shutter speed, which creates the perception of chronology in our memories. My brain, on the other hand, was not designed for chronology but for imaging. My shutter would open up completely and receive a massive amount of information all at the same time and then close very slowly, creating the phenomenon of overexposure before the shutter would close. When the shutter is open, I see every raindrop and even the spaces between the rain.

It appeared that my inability to filter out the massive data my brain was processing and my ability to retain massive amounts of information were directly interconnected. From a neurological perspective, my superpower was also my Achilles' heel. My strength was my struggle. For better or worse, the two were intertwined. It is said that our strengths are the shadows of our weaknesses. For me, this was certainly true. I have always been a person who has a thousand ideas a second. And although that can work wonders if you are in a room that needs problem solving, it is a nightmare when you are trying to turn your brain off. A thousand ideas a second—just take a moment and let that sink in.

How do you stop your brain from overwhelming you with unwanted thoughts and ideas? There would be days the onslaught inside my head would be paralyzing. Ideation is a wonderful gift to be given, but sometimes it's the gift that never stops giving. It would be impossible to count how many times Kim and I have lain in bed and she would break the silence by pleading with me, "Could you please turn your brain off? It's so loud in this room that I can't even sleep."

Some days it would be worse than others. On those days, I would crawl up into a ball in the corner of the room and beg my brain to stop, to give me some reprieve. Some days all you want inside your head is silence. I can tell you, as someone who has been on this journey, that you need to know your mind or else your very thoughts will drive you out of your mind.

I thought I was alone in the world with this battle. Just to know that someone else understood my struggle was enough to help me face it one more day. More than that, it let me know there was a way through, that maybe even, if only for a moment, I could take the madness and turn it into genius. At the very least, I could take the thousands upon ten thousand voices that were in my head and, like a conductor who is not overwhelmed by the sounds coming in his direction, orchestrate them into a beautiful symphony. Looking back on my life, this was perhaps my first great battle. This for me may have been the first step on my journey for the way of the warrior. I would either lose my mind or know my mind.

Around the age of twelve, I found myself sitting in a psychiatric chair looking at blotches of ink on a card and being asked, "What do you see?" This question was so much more profound than it seems. If I told the doctor what I saw, he would be able to see inside me. How we see the world is how we see ourselves. The warrior understands that their mind is both their greatest strength and their greatest danger. The warrior sees every raindrop and celebrates its beauty. The warrior sees the spaces between the raindrops and sees them as the way forward.

Making the Rain Dance

Have you ever stopped to listen to the rain? My wife, Kim, loves the rain. Whenever it rains, everything has to stop and I have to join her as she listens intently to the sound of every drop as it hits the tree branches, and the leaves that remain after winter, and after it hits the ground and bounces back up in a thousand tiny pieces. Actually, she hates getting wet, so she doesn't actually like the rain; she likes how the rain creates a sound that soothes her soul and calms her spirit.

If you listen carefully enough, you can hear the rain dancing. Yet when we speak of rain, we think of it as a whole and not the sum of its parts. But in some sense, both of those perceptions are accurate. There's a unity, almost a communal nature to rain, in which it moves in concert, each drop to the other. Still, every raindrop is unique and solitary and independent of all the others. The perfect metaphor for perhaps the most difficult and critical discipline for the warrior is that your thoughts are like a rainstorm. They are both the single thought of who you are and an endless array of thoughts crashing against your soul.

When I was young, this internal reality affected how I related to my external world. It was hard to listen to people because it was so loud inside my head. School seemed to move at a glacier's pace. All my thoughts moved at what seemed like light speed, or at least they moved me into imaginary worlds. Sometimes I would find myself drowning in my thoughts. I look back now and realize that I was ill-equipped to deal with the world around me, so I created an alternative world within me. I quickly became more comfortable in the world I imagined than in the world I lived in.

It shouldn't be possible to lose yourself inside yourself, but I have become convinced that this is the only place where you can be truly lost. If you're not careful, your thoughts can become more dangerous than a bullet to the head. The warrior knows that their imagination is not a place to escape but to create. The warrior retreats into themselves not to hide from the world but rather to prepare for it. There is no surer way to lose yourself than to spend your life thinking about yourself. When you fully know yourself, the focus of your mind moves toward serving others. To know yourself is to know the world.

According to the Laboratory of Neuro Imaging at the University of Southern California, the average human has around 48.6 thoughts per minute. That adds up to a total of almost seventy thousand thoughts per day,[52] meaning if you're on the lower end of the spectrum, you'll have about one thought every two seconds. If your brain is a bit more compulsive, you may have up to one thought every second. Imagine that—one thought every second. And I doubt that thought lasts only a second. And although the data on how many thoughts we have in a day is still more speculation than science, it is even more unclear how many thoughts we can hold in our minds at the same time. How many thoughts can go racing through our minds, moving through so quickly that we can't take hold of them? Yet every one of them finds its way to cut into the fabric of who we are.

When Kim and I were first married, I was still trying to work my way through the torrential rainstorms that flooded the inside of my brain. She found me this way only once or twice, but I would often sit in the corner in a fetal position, trying to get my brain under control. It's hard to explain what I was experiencing, but basically it felt like a barrage of endless thoughts ricocheting inside my head, refusing to be quiet.

Maybe this was the best thing that could happen to me—an almost crippling awareness that too many thoughts were happening at one time. It was in hearing every raindrop that I realized I needed to find a way to turn them into a cascade. If we as humans are so complex that these three pounds of gray matter can operate at such blinding speed that it causes computers to pale in comparison, how are we ever expected to find peace of mind?

It may seem completely counterintuitive, but I also know what it feels like to be paralyzed at the other end of the spectrum. I remember being nineteen years old and having no idea what to do with my life. I had barely graduated from high school. I had no hope of gaining admission into a college. I couldn't even imagine a future worth fighting for. I was drowning in meaninglessness, and it had become a daily struggle to simply survive.

Unfortunately, many of us are not struggling with too many thoughts and ideas; we are suffering from a mental atrophy that is the result of apathy, uncertainty, or fear. One of the curious things I have learned about the brain is that it is essentially a lazy muscle. That's why we are so teachable. Once we learn something, we don't want to unlearn it. Once we believe something, we don't want to unbelieve it.

The mental structure that makes us teachable gives us the same potential to become unteachable. If you think you already know everything, there is nothing left to learn. It is ironic that the most intelligent people are the most aware of how much they don't know. Genius isn't about what you know; it's about your insatiable curiosity for the unknown. If you are not careful, you can trap yourself inside a closed mind. You have no future because you are living in the past. You see the world as lacking opportunity because you are blind to the endless possibilities all around you. Arrogance makes the brain rigid; humility allows our minds to stay open.

While I was attending a seminar on neuroscience and cognitive development, it was stated that gratitude may be the most significant lubricant to mental acuity and adaptability. I wrote about this many years ago in my book *Uprising,* and only now is the most advanced neuroscience catching up to what Scripture taught us all along. I know this is harsh, but small-minded people will live small lives because they can survive only in a small world.

If you find yourself living in a world where there is only cynicism, negativity, and distrust, you need to realize that it's a world of your own making. There is a more beautiful world out there to be known, but you have to be able to see it. You have to want it. You must be willing to risk, to step outside of what you know, to live in a more extraordinary unknown.

We all know the old adage about why an elephant with all its power can be held in place by a small rope and peg. This is because elephants remember when they were babies and did not have the strength to pull the peg out of the ground. In short, elephants remain captive because their memories lie to them. They tell them that their past is their future—that what they experienced before will always be the reality that is before them.

Remember, your brain is inherently lazy. It will retreat to whatever previously set boundaries and patterns you have established from your past behavior. This is why it is so important to always try something new. People who travel have significantly higher IQs than people who do not. People who read authors with different perspectives become more open minded and empathetic. You can start with small things: try new foods, meet new people, learn a new language, consider a new idea, try a new approach.

In other words, break out of the routine you have established for yourself and force your mind to engage the new. This will begin to unlock opportunities and possibilities. This will open your mind to the beauty and wonder all around you.

The ultimate purpose of knowing your mind is not to be limited by it. The mind of the warrior is postured in humility and textured with gratitude, where it is most free.

Captivating Thoughts

Almost twenty-five years ago, I was invited to an event in the mountains of North Carolina. It was there that I first encountered a renowned theologian who over the past two decades has become one of the most influential voices coming out of New York City. I remember that after his brilliant presentation—and, frankly, being new to faith, I hadn't heard a lot of brilliant presentations—I risked asking him a question that must have seemed heretical to him but was painfully personal to me.

In the few moments that we were allowed, I asked him a question that might help me figure out how to bring seventy thousand thoughts a day into a common narrative. Because in truth, for me, it didn't feel like seventy thousand thoughts; it felt like seventy thousand voices screaming inside my head. I don't know how crowded it feels inside your head, but sometimes all the different voices are determined to tell you who you are. It can feel like an overcrowded elevator where there's not enough oxygen for everyone to breathe.

So I said to the theologian, "Scripture tells us that we are to take every thought captive to the obedience of Christ. This seems to be an impossibility. There are just too many thoughts to take captive." If you are having one thought every second, all you would do every second of your life is try to take that thought captive to the obedience of Christ. I asked him in that moment, "Is it possible that the only way to take thoughts captive is by the shaping of a mind-set or the creation of a worldview—that once you've shaped your worldview, then it guides your thoughts? That once you have established a mind-set, that mind-set filters your thoughts?"

I must have asked the question wrong, because I'll never forget his response. He said, "Be careful. It sounds like you're talking about mind control."

It sounds like you're talking about mind control. I've come to the conviction that he was more right than he could have ever known. Your mind-set controls your mind, and this can be both good and bad. If your construction of reality has been shaped subconsciously by the influence of others and the experiences of your own life, you may be under the control of others far more than you realize.

There are layers of language that describe this phenomenon. Sometimes the language you use is worldview. The concept of a worldview entered our language in the 1850s. It comes from a German word that is describing a comprehensive conception or image of the universe and of humanity's relation to it. Others talk about our mind-set, which is also fairly recent language, first used in the 1920s. And while worldview deals with our comprehensive view of reality, mind-set deals more with our personal attitude, intention, or disposition toward life.

When you know your mind, you begin to see that your worldview and your mind-set are inseparable. If your view of the universe is that it is generative, creative, and unlimited in its resources, you will have a mind-set of generosity and will engage life with open hands and profound optimism. If your worldview understands the universe to be the result of arbitrary chance or of mathematical determinism, your mind-set will filter out any proof that would support the contrary.

In the most practical sense, what matters most is how you see life. Your internal mind-set designs your external world. If you believe the world is full of possibilities, it is. If you believe the world is filled with fascinating people, you will find them. If you believe the future is waiting to be created, you will create the future that is waiting for you. If you believe in love, you will find love. If you believe in hope, you will find hope. And the reason you will find them is because you will bring them with you.

We don't simply find the world we are looking for; we create it. This is why the warrior must know their mind. Your mind is where your future is formed. If your mind-set is formed by fear and anger or by greed and envy, that's the only kind of world you will ever find. You will never fully understand that you found that world because you created it and compelled it to come.

The warrior trains their mind to know the good and beautiful and true. This is the war they fight within themselves, and this is the world they fight to create. We have a warm word for living in the past: *tradition*. In the theological world, it's known as *orthodoxy*, and in the world of science, it's simply called *truth*.

You cannot take every thought captive one thought at a time. This would lead to madness. You can capture your thoughts only by proactively creating the filter through which those thoughts are processed. To begin to take every thought captive, you must ask yourself, *Where did those thoughts come from, and how did they get into my head?* The process of taking every thought captive begins by identifying the source of your thoughts and the filter through which those thoughts are sent out or allowed in.

Mind of Your Own

We already know through our cognitive processes, such as selected sensory perception, that we are not aware of everything we see—that our brains filter out, without asking us permission, everything they assume is irrelevant for our survival. We see only what we need to see—except when we don't. There are those moments in which critical information has been filtered out because it was wrongly perceived as irrelevant.

The same holds true with the thoughts that rise out of our subconscious into our conscious minds. Your mind-set filters out information that disagrees with your view of reality. And if it doesn't filter it out, it distorts it to conform to your view of reality. The thoughts that your mind-set allows to move quickly through to your conscious mind are the ones that reaffirm already held beliefs and convictions.

The same researchers who assess that we have up to sixty thousand thoughts a day also assess that up to 80 percent of those thoughts can be negative and repetitive.[53] That would mean that forty-eight thousand negative thoughts come crashing into your brain every single day of your life. You may be aware of only half a dozen of them.

Maybe that would be a great exercise in self-awareness. Take a moment and write down every negative thought that comes to mind. Then write down every positive thought that holds your attention. Which seem to most naturally come to the surface for you?

The extreme version of mind control would cause you to no longer be able to think for yourself. The opposite version is to actually believe you can think for yourself, because you've never taken time to deconstruct your mind-set. You never even ask yourself the hard question, *How did I come to see the world this way?*

When the apostle Paul was writing to the Romans, he instructed them, "Do not conform to the pattern of this world, but be transformed by the renewing of your mind. Then you will be able to test and approve what God's will is—his good, pleasing and perfect will."[54] This may be one of the most commonly referred to passages in the Bible, yet we rarely know how to apply it. What does it mean to "conform to the pattern of this world"? Far too often this was denigrated to moralizing over a person's actions, but that's not at all that Paul was talking about. When the apostle speaks of not conforming to the pattern of this world, he's actually confronting our mind-sets. There is a pattern of thinking that is formed inside a person who does not believe in God. It is interesting that Paul sees the process of breaking free from conforming patterns as the transformation of the renewing of our minds. The warrior must see the world from a new perspective. The warrior sees life from a different vantage point. The way of the warrior is the path to a new mind-set. The warrior has a new mind.

It is no small thing that Paul says that only with this new mind can you become a new you. So often the will of God is described as something to be received rather than something that must be perceived. Paul tells us that when our minds are renewed, it is then and only then that we are able to test and approve what the will of God is. When we see the world from this new mind, we will see that God's intention for us is good and pleasing and perfect.

Imagine having an infinite number of futures right in front of you and each one of them is as easily accessible as the others. All you have to do is choose one. The challenge is that all of them are invisible to you and are perceivable only by the material that you bring into the moment. Historically, we have been taught to think of the will of God from a linear perspective. His will becomes more of a tightrope that we either walk on or fall off of. It's this kind of limited view of the future that causes us to speak in terms of God's perfect will and God's permissive will. Once you have fallen off the tightrope of his perfect will, all you are left with is a merciful version of a divine plan B. The future is more beautifully complex than that. It makes perfect sense that an infinite God would have an infinite number of beautiful futures awaiting us. In fact, one of the most reassuring promises in Scripture is that God can create the most beautiful future out of our imperfection and brokenness. When Paul says that we will be able to test and approve God's good, perfect will for our lives, we think of one path, one line, one road.

What if the future is far more complex and beautiful than this? What if there is an endless number of futures awaiting us but the portal through which we enter into those futures is shaped by the choices we make? Paul connects having a new mind with creating a new future. The future is not linear; it is dynamic. The future is not determined; it is created. This is why it is so critical to know your mind. It is in your mind that the future begins. It is through the transformation of your mind that you can usher in the future only God could have planned.

The only thing better than our imagining a better life is creating it. The only thing better than imagining a better world is creating it. The warrior understands that the world's best future will not come without a battle. You must fight for the future that you dream of. The warrior does not fight to hold on to the past but rather to take hold of the future. The future belongs to those with the courage to create it. This is the way of the warrior. The warrior remembers but does not look back. The future is coming from only one direction and that's forward. The warrior has learned that if their mind is lost in the past, they will lose their future.

Have you ever felt that there was an opportunity that you missed and you don't know how you didn't see it? It's almost as if we're color-blind, but the blindness is actually related to the future. It's not that you must choose a future; it's that you must choose *the* future.

Your mind-set is the filter through which you see your potential futures. If you enter into life with optimism and hope, you will see an endless number of futures filled with optimism and hope. You will see possibilities and opportunities all around you. You will see wonder and beauty. You won't see just one choice that could lead to a more beautiful future. The only thing that may overwhelm you or make you feel paralyzed is that you have so many good choices from which to choose. Wouldn't it be an amazing life if you had to keep saying no to extraordinary choices—to an alternative and beautiful future? So often we act as if there are only two choices for the future: a good one and a destructive one, the one that God chooses for us and the one we choose for ourselves.

I think the future is much more like the garden, where humanity's story began. We tend to focus on the two trees, but the garden was full of trees. One of the first commands of the Bible was for Adam and Eve to eat freely. They were allowed to eat from the fruit of any tree in the garden except for one. Most of the time, we act as if there is only one good choice and an endless number of choices that will destroy our lives. This is not how the story of the world began, and this is not how the story continues.

When your mind is shaped by hope, you do not see simply two paths; you see an endless number of paths filled with opportunity, possibility, and beauty. However, if your mind-set is shaped by cynicism or fear or doubt, then the only paths you see in front of you are the ones that are filled with pain and disappointment, with failure and hardship.

Have you ever considered that what you allow to shape your mind is what shapes your perception of the opportunities in front of you? That's why when you are full of fear, every possible future seems terrifying. That's why when you carry inside your soul wounding and brokenness, every potential future is fraught with disappointment and betrayal. Your mind-set shapes how you see reality, but more important, it shapes how you see your future.

How many futures can you see right now? Are they filled with joy, with friendship, with success and fulfillment? Or are they the kinds of futures you would do anything to avoid? I think why so many of us are paralyzed, why we hold on to the past and live trapped in the moment, is that we can't see our way out into different lives. We can't see our way through to better futures. It's important that we note that even though our mind-set filters the information that we receive consciously, it determines what information moves from our subconscious into our conscious minds. It also becomes like a telescope that points us to a very particular future, but what it allows us to see is not all that's available to us.

The hardest thing to do is convince someone who is overwhelmed with despair that there is actually a future and hope. One
of the most difficult things to do is convince someone who has been
heartbroken, who has lost at love, that there is a person out there who
will love them completely and will long for their love in return. It is
very difficult to help someone who has come to the end of a dream,
who feels devastated by failure, to realize there is a greater future waiting for them, that there is another dream waiting to be awakened.

One of the greatest gifts we can give others is to help them have
new eyes with which they can see their own selves, their own lives,
and their own future. Paul's words become more poignant: "Do not
be conformed to the pattern of this world. Do not allow your mind
to be shaped by any patterns that would steal from you the hope
that God created you to live in."[55]

A Mind for the Future

Whenever someone tells me they don't have faith, I ask them if they
have anything planned for tomorrow. Because if you have anything
planned for tomorrow and you don't have faith, that's the most absurd decision you've ever made. How can you plan something for
tomorrow when tomorrow doesn't exist? How can you plan something for a week from now or a month from now or a year from now
without faith? If you really didn't have faith, you would take all your
vacation time right away. After all, why would you leave it to the
future, which is not guaranteed? Now, that's an act of faith.

Faith shapes your mind-set. It shifts your perspective about your limits or the lack thereof. It's perplexing when someone puts their faith in something that seems absolutely absurd and then it comes to pass.

I remember watching Super Bowl LI. At one stage in the game, the New England Patriots were down about twenty-five points against the Atlanta Falcons. Every one of us in the room was certain that the game had already been decided by halftime except for one person: my son, Aaron. He never gave up on the Patriots. He seemed to somehow believe the entire time that they would come back and win. We thought he was ridiculous. Over time, though, you could just feel the entire emotion of the room shift as quarterback Tom Brady kept leading one successful drive after another. At the end of the game, the rest of us were stunned to have witnessed one of the greatest comebacks in Super Bowl history. But Aaron had been simply waiting for us in the future, for reality to catch up with faith.

We may call it economics, but Wall Street is an industry of faith. Education is completely built on faith. We pour into the lives of an emerging generation, believing that if they are well taught, they will create a better world. Imagine how it would shift your perspective of the future if you actually began to live by faith, if you allowed faith to shape your mind-set. This would radically change the way you would see every circumstance in your life. Even in the most difficult and painful times, you would see every moment as a promise that God would meet you there. You would never see anything in life as a dead end because you'd know that God would always guide you to a way through.

Faith changes our perceptions of the future. Faith always sees a way. In Hebrews we are told that faith is the substance of things unseen and the assurance of things hoped for.[56] I don't know about you, but I have found it's much easier to have confidence in things I have rather than things I hope for. In the same way, it's much easier to have assurance about things I can see than about things I cannot see.

When we have confidence in things hoped for, we are instantly connected to the future. Hope cannot exist in the past. That's called regret. Hope can exist only in the future. Faith connects us to the future. It also shifts the parameters of our limitations. When we have assurance in things seen, we are limited by what we have, by what we know, and by what we can prove. When we have assurance in things not seen, we now add to our resources everything that exists in the realm of mystery, uncertainty, and endless possibilities.

My wife and I were recently at a conference in Northern California called EG. It's a more intimate version of TED, bringing together some of the world's greatest thinkers, researchers, and explorers. I was pretty certain Kim and I would enjoy two days of anonymity, but within the first few hours someone recognized me as the pastor of Mosaic and impressed me with a question about the absurdity of faith.

The query was very specific: "So you believe that God made the sun stand still?" A small crowd had gathered. Before I could even answer the initial question specifically, there came a follow-up one: "There are people who believe the sun stood still and people who do not believe the sun stood still. What would you say would be the qualitative difference between those two kinds of people?"

I looked at him as if the answer was obvious. I told the small group listening, "I think it matters less whether you believe the sun stood still than whether you have such limited thinking that you believe that it's not possible. I prefer the mind-set that believes the sun could stand still because it is a mind-set of endless possibilities." The person who automatically eliminates that possibility is a person with limited thinking. I love that faith expands our imagination and opens us to a universe with endless possibilities.

It's the same with love. There may be no more dramatic shift in perspective than when we come to the conviction that the entire universe is created out of love—that everything exists because of love, that God is love, and that his primary motivation in all things is love. Once you believe the intention of the universe is to expand the love that God has graciously released upon all creation, it will change your view of everything. You cannot believe that God's will is good and pleasing and perfect if you do not believe that the unifying principle of the universe is love.

When you allow your mind-set to be shaped with the dynamic processes of faith, hope, and love, your mind-set becomes ever expanding. When your mind stream is informed by the endless opportunities visible only by faith, by the rich beauty and wonder visible only with hope, by the richness and depth available only through love, then the future becomes everything God ever intended it to be for you.

So my question for you is simple: When you look into the future, what do you see? The warrior must win the battle in their mind against fear, doubt, and hate and walk courageously into a future revealed only through faith, hope, and love.

The Warrior Owns Defeat

The warrior knows that honor is not found in the victory. Honor is found in the nobility of the battle. If the battle is not worthy of the warrior's life, there is no honor in its victory. In the same way, the warrior knows there is no dishonor in defeat. Failure and defeat are not the same. To fear defeat is to surrender victory. There is only a good fight and a good death for the one whose life is given to the noble. The warrior never claims victory for themselves but only for others. In the same way, the warrior never gives blame for defeat but owns it for themselves. The warrior owns defeat, and therefore defeat never owns the warrior. The warrior who lives and dies with honor enters eternity undefeated.

The ancient samurai understood that even in defeat there was an honorable death, for if you never lose your honor, you cannot die in defeat. Both in life and in death, the warrior never relinquishes their power. They do not place blame nor abdicate responsibility.

This is the life they have chosen. This is the path that called them forward. There is only defeat if you betray yourself and forsake your calling. The warrior's legend is that they cannot be defeated.

The warrior knows they are most powerful when they take ownership for everything entrusted to them, yet they claim ownership over nothing. The warrior takes complete responsibility while never holding tightly to anything. They take full responsibility without ever needing any praise. In this way, the warrior owns both everything and nothing.

Because the warrior lives with open hands, nothing can be taken from them. The warrior is free from all things and therefore is free to enjoy all things.

Everything is borrowed. Even those things that we consider our possessions will one day belong to someone else or perhaps to no one at all. That's why in most cases the concept of ownership is an illusion. Ownership is not about possession; it is about responsibility. What you own matters far less than what you take ownership for. What you take responsibility for is far more important than what you think you own.

One of the great traps on earth is to spend more of your time and energy trying to own things rather than owning your life. Your greatest stewardship is how you live the life you have been given. It is a strange thing that we can own something and abdicate ownership of ourselves. Without recognizing it, we all too often relinquish the ownership of our own lives to the slavery of another.

Whatever the circumstances, when we hold someone else responsible for our lives or for the condition of our lives, we are abdicating the responsibility that has been entrusted to us. We are far more compelled by possession than by responsibility. We want to own, but we don't want to take ownership.

If you have taken ownership of your life, you have come to know your own power. You don't stagger through life with a sense of powerlessness. You know who you are and that you are ultimately responsible for the future you create and the choices you make. Choosing doesn't just happen; it's how you make things happen.

The Freedom of Responsibility

Adam and Eve were placed in the middle of a garden and lived in what could only be described as paradise. In the garden, there were two trees that have become part of the infamous beginning of the human story: one tree that nurtured life, and one that would end it. Of course, God gave Adam and Eve a choice. Actually, God gave them endless choices.[57]

As we saw earlier, that command was to eat freely. There were an endless number of trees in the garden from which they were allowed to eat as much and as often as they desired. However, there was one tree that they were forbidden to eat from. Because man was created free, this tree had to exist. Without choice, there is no freedom. Without freedom, there is no choice. God instructed the first man and woman not to eat of this tree, because this choice would lead to their death. You would think the ominous nature of the warning would have been enough to keep them from it, but as we know, it was not. They ate of the tree and for the first time came to know shame.

Shortly afterward, God came to them, as I imagine he always did, but this time they hid because they were naked and afraid. God called to the man, and the man said, "I heard you in the garden, and I was afraid because I was naked; so I hid."[58]

The Creator asked the most curious of questions: "Who told you that you were naked? Have you eaten from the tree that I commanded you not to eat from?"[59]

The man's response was quite unexpected. Rather than taking responsibility for what he had just done, he threw Eve under the bus. There is a bit of comedic irony in his response. He says to God, "The woman you put here with me—she gave me some fruit from the tree, and I ate it."[60]

In one sentence, the man blames everyone else involved except himself. He says to God, "The woman you put here, God, it's your fault. I was doing great while I was here alone. You put her here, and your decision has led to my demise."

It's interesting to note that the man's first instinct was to blame God for the consequence of his own choice. Without missing a beat or wasting a breath, after blaming God, he blamed the woman: "She gave me some fruit from the tree. God, it's your fault. And if you are unwilling to take responsibility then I have a backup plan for you. It's the woman's fault. In fact, it is everyone's fault except my own. You put the woman here. She gave me the fruit from the tree. All I did was eat it."

Adam's entire response to God was one of abandonment of personal ownership and responsibility for his actions. He played the victim and painted himself a passive participant in the crisis he himself had created.

Then it seems God turned to the woman and asked her, "What is this you have done?"[61] I kind of feel sorry for her. The man was able to answer first, so she had no one left to blame. He had already blamed God and already blamed her and postured himself as an innocent bystander. She must have looked around and decided there was only one party left to blame. Her response: "The serpent deceived me, and I ate."[62] She had fewer people to blame, but instead of taking responsibility for her own actions, she blamed the snake. In a strange twist, the snake had no one to blame but had in fact done exactly what he'd intended.

If you're not familiar with the story of the two trees, it's important to understand that this was the moment in which humanity was introduced to death. What makes this exchange perplexing is that from every perceivable angle, the man and woman looked completely and fully alive. It's hard to know that you are dead when you don't know how to identify the symptoms. In one moment, humanity went from the fullness of life to mere existence, and the first symptoms of this change were shame and the birth of blame.

The symptoms of existence are visible through all human history and within the heart of every individual who has ever walked this earth. If humanity were fully alive, all we would know is a world filled with hope and joy and love and meaning. Every human action would be an expression of generosity and compassion and kindness. The symptoms of mere existence are evidenced in our deep sense of disconnection, desperate loneliness, and prevailing meaninglessness.

To not know love is to merely exist.

To not have hope is to merely exist.

To live without intention is a symptom that we have lost our lives and know only existence.

God had entrusted everything to the man and woman. He had placed everything under their authority. He had given them ownership—not possession but responsibility—over all creation. There was no question about who was responsible. There was no room for blame shifting. Yet neither the man nor the woman took responsibility for their actions. Neither of them owned their choices. Both of them acted as if they were powerless and merely victims of a more ominous force that they could not resist.

How difficult would it have been to have simply said, "It was my fault," and take responsibility? "You gave me stewardship over creation, and I betrayed your trust." Wouldn't it have been far nobler for the man to stand between God and the woman and say, "It was all on me. This is not on her"? Yet instead of standing as her shield, he threw her under the bus.

This was not simply the beginning of blame, nor the end of taking responsibility. It was the end of love. If Adam loved Eve more than he loved himself, he never would have made this choice or placed the blame on her. His instincts shifted from self-sacrifice to self-preservation.

Imagine being God in this moment, watching a creature you'd made in your image and likeness choose to protect himself rather than the one you had created for his love. Eve was unprotected because she was unloved. Adam acted in fear because he had lost the courage that only love can compel.

Then again, the woman had her opportunity for ownership as well. After she watched her husband cower and abdicate responsibility for his choice, she could've taken responsibility for handing him the fruit. She could have stood before God and said, "I listened to the wrong voice. I made the wrong choice. Do with me as you will. This is on me." But she didn't do that either.

It is not incidental that one of the first consequences of the Fall is the abdication of personal responsibility for our actions. To blame others is an act of cowardice. We blame in an attempt to hide our shame. This is not the way of the warrior. The warrior understands that to blame is not simply an abdication of responsibility but a relinquishing of power. You cannot change what you do not take responsibility for. When you blame someone else, you become dependent on that individual to solve your problem and change your circumstance. After all, if it is that person's fault, then he or she is the only one who has the power to change your condition.

The Weight of Responsibility

Jesus once told a story that bears similar circumstances. Speaking of the kingdom of God, he told the story of a master who left three of his servants in charge of different portions of his wealth.[63] One servant was given five talents, another two talents, and another one talent. A talent, during the days of the Roman Empire, was a measure of weight, not a specific value. A talent would weigh about seventy-five pounds.[64] So you could be entrusted with seventy-five pounds of gold or seventy-five pounds of silver or seventy-five pounds of copper. Though the weight would be the same, the value would be dramatically different.

After the master had divided his wealth between them, entrusting each of them with an amount that matched his ability, he left on a great journey. During his absence, each servant was left to his own devices to do with the master's wealth as he saw fit. In other words, they were left with endless possibilities. The servants had probably never known such great wealth. Even the one with only one talent would have had in his possession a relative value of almost $1.5 million.[65]

What would you have done with $1.5 million? Over the course of many years, how would you have invested it? What choices would you have made to optimize the wealth entrusted to you? How would you have increased your master's wealth and exceeded his expectations upon his return?

Eventually there came a day when the master returned to take account of what he had entrusted to his servants. I suppose some of you are familiar with the outcome. The one who had been given five talents returned to his master ten. The one who had been entrusted with two talents had doubled his account to four. But the one who had been given one talent had made a decision to bury his resources and gave in return to the master only what had been given to him.

The same question comes crashing into my mind when I think about both the man in the garden and the man who buried his talent: Why would you squander such an extraordinarily good opportunity?

Through this parable, Jesus provides a perfect example of why ownership is not about taking possession of what's in front of you but about taking responsibility for what has been entrusted to you. The men who multiplied the master's wealth were not the owners of that wealth, but they did take ownership of it.

When the one-talent servant explained to his master why he had buried his talent, we observe the very same pattern as we found with Adam and Eve: "Master, I knew that you are a hard man, harvesting where you have not sown and gathering where you have not scattered seed."[66] His knee-jerk response was to blame the master for his lack of courage, initiative, and ambition. He basically said to him, "The way you are is the reason I am the way I am." There is a striking contrast between the one-talent servant and his two peers. The other servants let us know the incredible potential that was available during their master's absence, but the man who buried his talent could not see what he'd squandered.

When you blame others, when you abdicate responsibility for your life, you become powerless to change it. Growing that talent was completely the servant's responsibility, yet he was certain it was

the master's fault that he had failed. There is an unexpected relationship between blame and fear. Right after he blamed the master,
he continued by explaining, "I was afraid and went out and hid
your gold in the ground."

When you blame others for your failure, you become powerless
to change the world around you. You begin to live your life filled
with fear, paralyzed by uncertainty and embittered by a sense of
victimization. Fear may cause you to abdicate responsibility, but the
abdication of responsibility will most certainly cause you to live in
fear.

Ownership begins by owning your choices, by taking responsibility for your own life, and by making decisions to stop blaming
others and finding someone else to hold at fault. It may seem counterintuitive, but there may be nothing more empowering than taking responsibility for your life. Trusting God is not an abdication of
responsibility; it is an embracing of it.

The problem began with Adam and Eve. They didn't have the
luxury of having parents to blame. They had the perfect environment in which to make the best choices. For the rest of us, it's far
more complicated than that. Yet although the world is filled with
chaos and turmoil and making the right choice seems infinitely
more complicated now than in the garden, we must not be de-
terred. We have been entrusted with the power of choice. Those
things we would entrust to only God he has entrusted to us. It is
still in our power to create a better world. The fate of humanity's
future has been placed in our hands. We must never abdicate re-

sponsibility, for with it comes endless possibilities. The future awaits those with the courage to create it. Never forget that when you own defeat, it can never own you. So take ownership of your life, your future, and the world around you, for you can change only what you own.

No-Fault Policy

Sometimes we feel paralyzed by a past we didn't choose. We find ourselves broken and even traumatized by things that happened to us and not because of us. I have known way too many people who were carrying the weight of their pasts while trying to walk into new futures. From actions of neglect and abuse, violence and addiction, abandonment and mistreatment, there are many legitimate reasons people struggle to re-create themselves. We bear so many wounds that seem to make healing elusive.

I would never discount the devastating effects of wounds not bought but given. You had no choice about where you were born or to what family you were born into. I completely understand why so many people carry not only wounds but bitterness like a noose around the neck. It is not easy to convince someone to forgive when there is no contrition from the offender. It may be one of the most difficult things in this world to let go of bitterness when it has been the only dam holding back the tears.

Taking responsibility when something is your fault makes perfect sense, but it's a tough pill to swallow that you need to take ownership over your circumstances even when they're not your fault. Here is the hard reality: even if it's not your fault, it's still your responsibility.

Though the wounding wasn't your fault, the healing is your responsibility.

Though your past may not be your fault, your future is your responsibility.

Though their choices were not your fault, your choices are your responsibility.

Don't let those who are at fault keep their hold on your life by relinquishing your power to change and to be free of them. Bitterness is how your soul lets you know they still have power over you. Hatred traps the poison inside you. Only love and forgiveness allow you the power to move forward.

Anger is not your strength; intention is. Every person you have not forgiven, everything in the past that holds you, has stolen a part of who you are. One of the greatest battles of the warrior is to reclaim the territories of the soul.

We are reminded by Paul that we have been bought with a price and within us there is great treasure. The servant who buried the talent thought it was enough to say to the master, "I hid your gold in the ground. See, here is what belongs to you."[67] He had convinced himself that all he was responsible for was what had been handed to him. The truth is that we are responsible for far more than what we have been given; we are responsible for what could have been done with all that we have been entrusted with.

Response Ability

There is a relationship between personal responsibility and risk. One of the curious things about people is that we have an unexpected and extreme variation when it comes to the way we perceive ourselves in relationship to personal responsibility. When they're facing failure, some instinctively assess and attribute blame to outside forces: *It was the economy. It was management. It was someone else.*

Then there are others who relate to risk from a polar opposite. When they are assessing failure, their perspective is completely internal: *I failed to make the right choices. I didn't work hard enough. I lacked the talent to pull this off.* These assessments are less rooted in reality than in psychology. It's less about what is real than how we perceive reality.

The person who is more likely to blame outside factors usually has a higher sense of self-worth and confidence: *Of course, the problem wasn't me. I'm awesome.* When a person takes a high degree of responsibility for failure, they tend to have a less elevated sense of self and consider their success more the result of hard work than of talent.

So on this spectrum, there is an unexpected relationship between ownership and risk. When a person has high self-confidence yet takes minimal personal ownership for failure, that person will most likely become a low risk taker. You would intuitively think that the person who perceives himself as more talented and less responsible for failure would be the higher risk taker. But what's been found time and time again is that a high view of self, coupled with low personal responsibility for failure, can diminish a person's ability to take necessary risks and embrace challenges that do not guarantee success. A more grounded sense of self with high personal responsibility for failure postures a person to have higher resiliency and greater courage when facing necessary challenges.

You would in turn also conclude that the person who sees himself as less talented, who sees success as the outcome of his hard work and takes high personal responsibility for failure, would be low risk. But the opposite is true. When you take personal responsibility for failure, you actually gain power rather than lose it. If it was your fault, if it's your failure, you have the power to change the result. If it wasn't your fault, if you have no relationship to the failure, you are powerless to change both the outcome and the possibility for success.

You can hear this language all the time when you listen to certain professional athletes during interviews. Assuming they're on the losing team, they will blame the lineup of players on their team. However, if they win, they're likely to claim it is further evidence of their greatness. They are always responsible for the victory and never responsible for the defeat. They take ownership for success but never for failure.

The same dynamic can be observed when an athlete is involved in an individual sport. If they lose, they may claim it's because of an injury or weather conditions or another external variable. If they win, they of course claim it's further evidence of their personal greatness. Many times this is why if a world-class athlete in an individual sport does not live up to expectations, they will immediately fire their coach. They figure someone is to blame, and the one certain thing is that it is not their own fault.

I recently met with a business owner, who shared with me how they were struggling through the loss of employees that were leaving the company. Their industry is one that lends itself toward personal friendships and relationships among people who work together. The owner felt a profound sense of betrayal, not just because the employees chose to leave them but because each time they left, they would blame the owners for creating a negative environment. I reminded the owner of how over the years when those same employees worked for other companies, each time they left, they created negative scenarios to justify their leaving.

When you have a high self-image with a low relationship to personal responsibility, you have to create a scenario in which someone or something else is to blame. The important thing to remember is not that you need to have a lower view of yourself (although that may be true too) but that your power comes in taking personal responsibility for your life.

The way of the warrior is a path toward ownership. The warrior takes responsibility for their life, their actions, and the world around them. The warrior knows that they own nothing, so they can risk everything. The warrior knows that the measure of their success is not in the outcome but in the intention. The courage to face the challenge is the victory. The warrior is not afraid to be exposed by defeat. Defeat does not diminish the heart of the warrior, for they do not fight for their own fame but for the freedom of others.

If your view of yourself is greater than what reality can bear, you will choose to protect yourself from great risks because you cannot bear the blunt-force trauma of failure. If you know that failure is a temporary condition and believe hard work will see you through, you're more likely to take bigger risks. If your practice in life is taking great risks, you are all too familiar with the impact of failure. Ironically, if failure is not an option, neither is taking risks. Failure is an inevitable ingredient of success. And because you know that, you know that failure is not terminal.

Years ago, we at Mosaic had a massive breakdown at one of our events. The next day all the leaders of all the teams met to assess the breakdown. I remember asking for clarification and asking what I thought was a pretty simple question: "Who is responsible for this particular area where the breakdown happened?"

One by one, everyone in the room told me it was not their responsibility. It was a strange and surreal moment to be sitting in a room full of executives where apparently not one of them was responsible for the principal item on our agenda.

I paused for a moment, took a deep breath to think it over, and then gave everyone an assignment: "I want you to go find the person responsible for this so I can hire them, because they are the only person who should be in this room."

If you're not responsible for a problem, you don't have the power to fix it. Find the person who takes responsibility and you've found the person who has the power to bring change. You cannot own the moment if you do not take ownership. The warrior may never own anything but is responsible for the things that matter most. This is the way of the warrior.

The Warrior Harnesses Their Strength

The warrior knows their power. Even in defeat, the warrior is never powerless. Even when they are weak, the warrior knows their true strength. The warrior has a fire within that always burns brightly even in the darkest moments. Yet the warrior knows that the fire burns only if there is more wood to be consumed. The warrior understands the relationship between wood and fire and knows that the soul is a fire that must be fed to burn brightly. The warrior has learned how to harness their strength, focus their power, and replenish their energy. It is in this practice that the warrior becomes like a force of nature. The warrior always fuels the fire of their soul.

To survive a long winter, the warrior goes out morning by morning to secure enough wood to keep the fires burning within their shelter. They understand that the fire is life. If the fire goes out, the cold will overtake them, but wood keeps the fire burning. The warrior is the one who must feed the fire. There are some questions you must answer: What is it that feeds the fire within you? What is it that feeds your soul? What is the wood that you must work hard to gather to ensure that your fire does not go out?

The wood is not the same for everyone, though there are certain things that fuel us all. You will know the wood of your soul when your fire diminishes in its absence and when your fire intensifies in its presence. To identify your wood, the fuel to your fire, you must be mindful of what makes you feel most fully alive. What is it that ignites your passions? What are the moments in which you feel most energized?

The warrior finds their greatest strength when they love to live and live to love.

Love is the warrior's greatest strength. When we love our lives, we are inspired, encouraged, and energized to face even life's greatest challenges. To find your strength, you must know the source of your power and recognize where your energy comes from. At our most basic level, humans are energy wrapped up in skin. We were not designed for lethargy, we were not made for apathy, and we were certainly not created for mediocrity. The warrior knows how to harness their energy and replenish it for the next great battle ahead.

I live in a city where people don't talk a lot about God but instead talk a lot about energy. In fact, the use of the word *energy* here in Los Angeles has almost become a cliché. I cannot tell you how many times I have had people, usually from the entertainment industry, come up to me and open with "I love your energy." My wife, who grew up in the mountains of North Carolina, hates everything about the language of energy. I think it frustrates her that people give credit to an inanimate force rather than a personal Creator. But for me, energy has been a point of focus for nearly forty years. Although there may be individuals who use the word *energy* in trite or empty ways, there is an entirely new wellness industry that has come to understand it as a source of health, healing, and strength.

Some of my interest in energy has been very personal. Many years ago, my mom bought me my first nice watch. It was an elegant but simple Gucci timepiece. I remember feeling that the gift was so extravagant. Looking back now, I realize that it cost a few hundred dollars, but at that time in my life, that was a month's rent. It was only a few weeks after I had the watch and had worn it proudly every day that it stopped ticking. This watch was supposed to be of the highest quality, and suddenly I found it less reliable than a ten-dollar drugstore watch. I was both surprised and frustrated.

I took the timepiece to a watch repair shop. The employees checked the battery, and there was nothing wrong with it. In fact, when they went to work on the watch, it was running just fine. Of course, they changed the battery anyway. They had to charge me for something. I left a little bit confused, but I was also happy that my watch was not defective.

A week or two later, it stopped running again, so I repeated the process. I took my watch back to the shop. They checked the battery and changed it even though it was fine. The watch worked perfectly until, of course, I wore it for another week or two.

It was then that I began to entertain a bizarre concept: perhaps the problem was not the watch, but me. So I began to test the theory. I would wear the watch for a few days, and it would stop. I would put it in one of my drawers, and then a few days later it would be working perfectly again. After a few days of watching it keep time perfectly on the top of my dresser, I would wear it again, and it would stop.

I finally confirmed my theory by buying a second watch. To my surprise, the second watch had the same reaction as the first. After I wore it a few days, it stopped keeping time. So I began to alternate watches, and when one stopped, I switched to the other. I began to research widely and discovered that although it's rare, there are a handful of people around the world who can't wear watches because every watch they try dies. This phenomenon, as weird as it sounds, is due to the high electrical currents in some people's bodies. Depending on the level of electrical currents in your body or if you have been exposed to high volumes of electricity, you can literally interfere with the inner workings inside your watch. It sounds kind of insane that one of the top five reasons for why a watch has stopped is that certain human beings emit high electrical currents.[68] I wouldn't believe this except that it happens to me every single time. I can share with you only my personal experience. For years I was unable to wear a watch for more than a few days at a time. On the upside, it launched me into my hobby of collecting watches— this way I always have a working watch to bring into rotation.

At one point in my life, I found myself having the same experience with our old-school computers. It is not insignificant that a human being can carry so much energy that it can literally shut down a computer.

The most frustrating aspect of this is how often the security alarms at airports go off when I walk through the metal detectors. Since 2001 my traveling handle has been "random search." On one of my more recent trips, I asked the TSA agent why it is that the alarms constantly go off when I go through. He explained that they are set to identify higher electrical frequencies, and if you happen to have a higher electrical frequency, you set it off.

All this is to explain why I have had such a fascination with energy on a personal level and why, even when the language of energy has not been commonly used in conversations of our faith journey, it's more important than you may know. You don't simply have energy; you *are* energy.

E = MCMANUS^2

Probably the most popular and significant contribution that Albert Einstein made to modern science is his formula E=mc². Einstein's theory of special relativity states that the increase of the relativistic mass (m) of a body comes from the energy of motion of the body, which is kinetic energy (E) divided by the speed of light squared (c²).[69] Basically, he explained the relationship between mass and energy: energy equals mass multiplied by the speed of light squared.

In practical terms, the less energy, the more solid the mass. The more energy, the more fluid and dynamic the mass. In other words, a rock creates less energy than a river. For our purpose, an apathetic person has less energy than a person filled with passion. Wood has the potential of energy. Fire activates the energy within the wood. I have also just seen $E=mc^2$ as an abbreviation for Erwin McManus.

But what Einstein came to understand about the universe has as much significance for our personal lives as it does for an understanding of reality. Humans once understood mass and energy as two different things. It would have been seen as superstition to understand that the material that makes a ship is of the same essence as the material that makes the ocean. In many ways science is now more unbelievable than magic was three thousand years ago. This is captured in the idea that energy equals the sum total of mass in relationship to the speed of light in a vacuum. Or to summarize, energy and matter are two different forms of the same thing. It seems like magic that energy and matter are two different forms of the same thing, but science is sometimes stranger than fiction.

The way my simple mind translates all this is by realizing that coal is made of the same material as a fire. Coal simply is less motivated, or to be more specific, less energized. It also means that, although we know that energy cannot be destroyed or created, it can be released or contained. So the potential of an object in stasis may be far more dynamic than it appears if the proper heat is applied. For instance, coal contains within it tremendous energy for heated power and that actually turns into thermal energy when it is set on fire. What I want to share with you next may seem figurative, but it is actually more literal than you may know. You are born a piece of coal; you must become a fire. This is part of the warrior's journey.

To find the fire that burns within you is central to the way of the warrior.

I see the contrast every day, not only here in Los Angeles but also as I travel around the world. I meet people from every walk of life who seem to have endless energy for what they do. Their chosen fields are often as varied and unexpected as is humanly possible. Some are doctors, some architects, some painters, some dancers. Others are chefs or baristas or teachers or researchers.

Although their professions may have nothing in common, their labors have this one thing in common: they have endless energy for what they are doing. Their energy materializes itself in hard work, determination, resilience, excellence, and passion. Surprisingly, the same passion that they demonstrate at work affects every aspect of their lives. Sometimes their passion is all-consuming; they love their work and neglect their relationships. They are driven to create great art and seem to have no interest in creating great wealth. Some of the greatest works this world has ever seen were created by individuals with an all-consuming passion.

There are others who carry the same level of intensity, who express the same level of passion, but that passion is not isolated to a singular focus, but to life itself. These people are passionate about their work and passionate about their family and passionate about experiencing the beauty and wonder of life. They, too, bring an endless energy to everything they do, but their energy is less focused on what they do than on who they are. They have found the secret to being fully alive. They have also learned that energy expended must also be renewed. They have discovered the importance of caring for their private worlds and have recognized that their true strength comes from within. They know that to release more energy than they receive is a dangerous thing.

The warrior knows that they are not the ultimate source of their own strength. They know that the fire within them can go out if it is not cared for properly. But we are designed to live with passion. There is a default mode we can surrender to where we simply just exist, paralyzed by apathy or despair or discouragement. It may seem as if fear is a fuel to the fire, but in the end, all it does is diminish it. Fear consumes our energy, whereas faith restores it. When you live by faith, you find energy to live your life at full strength.

The warrior also knows that the fire within them can become a destructive force. The fire within can be stoked with the wrong wood when we are consumed with anger, envy, bitterness, jealousy, or hatred. The fire destroys not only our own souls but also the lives of those who come within the range of our flames. The warrior knows the danger of this fire and understands that it can be consumed only by a greater fire. When Jesus tells us that the most important commands from God are to love him with all our hearts, souls, minds, and strength and to love our neighbor as ourselves, they are mandates to know God as the all-consuming fire that burns within our souls.

Energy Grid

Few people here in Los Angeles have accomplished as much as my friend Mark Burnett. I once asked him what the number one characteristic is that he looks for when hiring key staff members. Without hesitation he answered, "Energy."

It shouldn't have surprised me, because Mark is one of the most energetic people I have ever known. It is not an exaggeration to say that when Mark Burnett is in the room, it is electric. It's funny to recall the first time I ever met him. I had just spoken at a conference, and as I walked off the stage, he said to me, "You have so much energy." Now knowing him better, I take that as his greatest compliment. This was no cliché; this was a genuine observation from a person whose own energy I deeply admire.

When you see a small child who is out of control, you might describe them as being full of energy. Certainly as a parent I have seen that different children have different levels of energy. Some of this is clearly genetic, yet a great aspect of our energy is connected to how we approach life and whether we have found a life that energizes us.

I want to be perfectly transparent: I don't always have endless energy. In fact, even as I write these words, I feel an exhaustion that has drilled its way to the core of my bones. I am really tired. Not Olympic athlete kind of tired, but that kind of weariness of the soul that makes you feel as if you're drowning in a black hole of exhaustion. Have you ever been there?

It is one thing to revel in a moment in which you have boundless energy, but that is not the measure of your strength. The warrior knows their strength only when standing in their weakness. That is why it's critical to assess what things in your life bring you energy and what steals it away. Our need for energy in order for us to live at an optimal level has become a common part of our everyday language.

Every morning millions of people wake up with one goal: to get that first cup of coffee that will give them the strength to get to their second cup of coffee. And while coffee may work well as your addiction, it is much more than that. Coffee, at its essence, is concentrated energy classified as caffeine. That orange juice you drank is energy. In fact everything you consume is energy.

Today we have an entire industry developed around the convenient consumption of energy. We have energy drinks and energy bars and even energy coaches. We have all learned the hard lesson that a child must never be given unfettered access to candy. Sugar is pure energy. We've also come to understand the relationship of energy to our physical health.

If you consume more energy than you expend, your body begins to store that energy as fat. Over the past few years, an endless number of programs and strategies have emerged for weight loss. Yet there's one simple formula that will always remain true: if you expend more energy than you consume, you will lose weight. If you consume more energy than you expend, you will gain weight. You are both a conduit of energy and a container of energy. And as perplexing as it may seem, even if you have chosen a life of lethargy, you are still at your core a ball of energy.

So how can it be that we *are* energy and can live unenergized lives? Have you ever tried to start a fire with wet wood or wet coals? The material that would normally burn easily and brightly loses its capacity to produce heat and create fire. There are conditions of the human spirit that steal from us not only our energy but our passion and desire to live life fully.

The warrior knows that the type of fuel that feeds their soul affects the fire that burns within them. Sometimes the fire is diminished, and sometimes it is misdirected. The warrior chooses the right fuel for their fire. The warrior knows that their heart is the furnace. The warrior knows that their passion is their source of strength. The warrior knows this one truth: if they lose their fire, they lose their strength.

Nothing will steal our strength like living lives we do not love. To pursue what we love is to be energized for life. If we cannot find the energy to live, we have not found love worth living for. Warriors have found boundless energy, for they have found boundless love. There is a direct relationship between what we are doing and the energy we have to do it. Everyone has an energy grid. The way we store energy is through our desires, values, passions, hopes, dreams, and aspirations, and ultimately our greatest capacity for energy storage is through what we love.

Rolling Blackouts

I have always found it unsettling that people can actually live their lives without passion. Over many years of working with leaders and mentoring potential ones, I have come to realize that people do not all bring the same level of energy with them. I have also come to know that even within our own lives, we each can experience massive variance in the amount of energy we feel or have available to engage life's greatest challenges and crises.

I remember a few years ago when I had been traveling for about two weeks and it was my first night home. I walked in the door, and just after I said hello, Kim responded with "Would you mind taking out the garbage?" After decades of marriage, I should have been able to translate that to its original meaning: *I'm so happy you're home. I love you, and I need your help so badly, more than words could ever express.* That, for those of you who can't read between the lines, was everything she was saying when she said, "Would you take out the garbage?"

My response, though, was less than I would have hoped for myself. I looked at her, frustrated and exhausted from my long journey, and said, "I just walked in the door. I'm really tired. Could you just let me rest for a while?" She immediately felt terrible and said, "Of course. I'm sorry. Just sit down and catch your breath."

Then a few minutes passed, and one of my friends gave me a call. He said they had a basketball gym available and a bunch of the guys were going to go play ball and wanted to know if I could jump in. I immediately knew that I was in a tenuous situation, so I said, "Let me give you a call back. I need to ask Kim if it would be okay if I go." I want to add a little footnote here. I don't need my wife's permission to go play basketball, but I do need it if I want to be happy and live a long and fruitful life.

I remember walking cautiously over in Kim's direction. I think she was cooking something. I said, "Honey, after I take out the garbage, I was wondering if I could go play basketball with the guys." I could see the fire in her eyes.

She said, "Oh no, I would never let you do that. You're so tired. You're way too tired to go play basketball. You don't even have the energy to take out the garbage. You just sit down and rest."

I can't really explain what happened. I was exhausted when she asked me to take out the garbage, but suddenly I was filled with energy, enough energy to play basketball and take out the garbage. She should have seen this as nothing short of a miracle, a gift from God.

Now, you might think that I was being selective, but actually something unique was happening. The things we love to do energize us; the things we do not enjoy doing cost us energy. It goes much further than the conflict between taking out the garbage and playing basketball. Every day of your life, you either choose to give yourself to those things that give you energy or you choose to give yourself to those things that cost you energy.

In the nearly thirty years that we have lived in Los Angeles, we have faced numerous energy crises across the state of California. Two phrases that I have become familiar with are *brownouts* and *rolling blackouts*. With the first, you have limited access to energy. With the second, you experience temporary losses of energy. During those periods, we were constantly reminded that it is possible to expend more energy than you actually have. We experienced similar conditions in Beirut, where the loss of energy often came without notice and at the most inconvenient times.

If we are not careful, we can experience the same phenomenon in our personal lives. Every day we make choices to conserve energy, expend energy, consume energy, and restore energy. Even when we are energized by life, it will still deplete us of energy. The things that energize us can also exhaust us.

Energizing and exhausting are not diametrically opposed. The things that give you energy also cost you energy, but that cost has a return. The things that energize you the most might actually cost you the most energy. They might be the hardest things that you do. They might be the most difficult challenges in your life. But when they are energizing, you do not find yourself in a deficit of energy, because whatever it costs you, the return is greater.

I love playing basketball, and I can say that it genuinely energizes me. It also leaves me absolutely exhausted and depleted of energy. I love writing books. I'm always energized when I tackle a new project, and it always leaves me both exhilarated and exhausted. When my kids were five and eight years old, they were the most adorable creatures on the planet. Nothing brought me greater joy than spending time with them and enjoying their endless energy. They were also exhausting. And I think it's fair to say that parenting may be the most difficult job in the world.

Just because you love something doesn't mean it doesn't cost you something. In fact the opposite can be true. You may be so passionate about a project that you give every ounce of energy that you have to it. The difference between those things that energize us, that cost us energy, and those things that steal our energy is that one is a result of a creative process and the other simply consumes our strength without benefit.

When I'm doing accounting, there is nothing about it that energizes me. When I have to deal with a staff member who's not executing at the expected level, it sucks the life out of me. Worry steals energy; fear steals energy; anger steals energy. Each in its own way creates a negative energy, what you might call a dark energy. It's like a black hole that consumes all the energy within your soul. Even good things that you were not meant to do can steal your energy. Certainly, living a life without purpose or engaging in work that you find meaningless will rob you of all the energy you need to live.

Some of us have become accustomed to living with "rolling blackouts." We go to work with a deficit of energy and live for the weekends, when we can pursue our passions. Isn't that the tragedy of why we "thank God it's Friday"? What a shame to work five days simply so that we can live two.

When you find yourself taking on projects or responsibilities for which you are not passionate, you will need to find a way to replenish the energy that you lost fulfilling those responsibilities. Ironically, this is why you must choose your battles carefully. If you fight a battle that actually doesn't matter to you, it will steal your strength. The warrior finds their strength because they fight only battles that matter.

Emotional Energy

Does your life energize you, or does it steal every ounce of strength you need simply to exist? In my experience, most of us experience life in unrealistic extremes. We either love our lives or hate them.

We either have lives we long for or long for different ones completely. We are either completely energized by the lives we have or
completely drained by them. We experience life in extremes, but
that's not the reality in which we live.

Hopefully you can find *something* to love even about the things
you hate. Even when people hate their jobs, they often find a way to
compensate by living the lives they love on the weekends. The problem is that it is impossible to segment your life on a permanent basis.
If you hate your job but love your marriage, eventually one will affect, and infect, the other. If you are unhappy in your relationships,
that unhappiness will begin to affect every other area of your life.

Negative emotions such as bitterness, unforgiveness, jealousy,
envy, and even greed will send your energy in a direction that does
not replenish your soul but in fact leaves you feeling lifeless and
empty. But it's not just negative emotions. You were never intended
to live life in neutral. To live a life that leaves you feeling indifferent
or apathetic is the path to a slow death. If getting up in the morning
is a struggle and you find yourself lacking the energy to engage life
fully, you can be certain that you are not living the life you were
created to live.

You are created to live a life of passion and compassion. When
you live a life of passion, it moves you to action. When you live a life
of compassion, it moves you beyond yourself into a life of service.
Negative emotions turn all your energy inward and you become an
emotional black hole. When you live a life of passion, you harness
your energy to be fully engaged in the creative process called life.

The more passion you have for something, the more energy you have to give to it. Those who seem to have boundless energy are the ones living their lives for their deepest passion. Where then does passion come from? Passion is love on fire. This is why the warrior knows this to be true—that love is the most powerful force in the world, that love is the warrior's greatest strength, that the way of the warrior is always love.

The warrior has mastery over their internal world. The warrior understands the process required to expend, preserve, and renew their energy. They know that their energy flows out of their passions, that their passion must flow out of love, that it is love that gives them ultimate joy, and that it is joy in which they find their strength. The way of the warrior has no room for anger or hate or violence. Those are the emotions of weaker men. The strength of the warrior comes not in hate but in love, not in anger but in joy, not in greed but in passion.

The warrior who has found ultimate joy can overcome anything. They have learned that the struggles of life are more than one can bear without joy. Scripture tells us that the joy of the Lord is our strength.[70] For all the battles we will fight, for all the struggles we will face, for all the wounds we will bear, only those people who are full of joy will find the strength to rise above them. To live a life of passion fueled by love and joy is to be fully alive.

Negative emotions pose as fuel or passion. And although they do cause you to burn, they do not lead you to create but rather to destroy. Anger can look like passion; hate can look like intention;

greed can look like motivation. Dark emotions such as hate, anger, and greed redirect energy into a destructive force. In fact all they do is steal your future and turn your soul not into a fire but a pit of ashes.

I was born in San Salvador, El Salvador. I came to the States as a child and was unable to return to my homeland for many years because of my country's history of violence. Most of the world knows El Salvador as a land of war and endless revolutions. Only out of a history that has known nothing but war and violence could an expression of our inhumanity have been created in the likes of the international criminal gang MS-13. Children with so much promise and potential, young men with incredible intelligence and talent facing hopeless futures and fueled by rage and greed, became the founders of one of the world's most violent and inhumane gangs. Negative emotions can make us forces, but no matter how much power we may acquire, it will never turn us into creative forces. Movements born out of anger, hatred, fear, or greed only harness our energy to make us destructive forces.

There are other negative emotions that move us not into a pattern of destructiveness but one of lethargy and apathy. Nothing will steal your energy like worry and fear. Worry consumes your energy without productivity. I have spent too many moments of my life worrying, far more than I would ever care to admit, yet I can say without exception that my worry has never made anything better. Worry is a waste of energy. Emotions such as anxiety and stress are the result of unharnessed energy misdirected by our fears and doubts. Fear feels like a fire except that it does not create light, only darkness. When we are afraid, our energy is consumed by the darkness of our souls. Fear is like a black hole consuming all the light. It steals all our energy and leaves us powerless.

It is the same with doubt. When you doubt, you hesitate. When the warrior hesitates, he faces certain defeat. We are told that "one who doubts is like a wave of the sea, blown and tossed by the wind. That person should not expect to receive anything from the Lord. Such a person is double-minded and unstable in all they do."[71]

When you doubt, your energy wars against itself. It becomes unharnessed and unfocused and loses its power. There is a strength that comes when you have confidence that even if you fail, you've given yourself to the right battle. We spend too much of our lives trying to make sure we are right about the what, the where, the when, and the how, and too little time making sure we are right about the why. The why is the one battle you need to be right about. This is the one area you cannot afford to be wrong about. You can be uncertain about everything else, but you need to know your why.

Your why is the light that will guide your way.

Your why is the light that moves you forward in the darkness.

Your why is why you are alive.

If you don't know your why, you will merely exist and not live. Your why is your truth, and when you know the truth, it sets you free. When you know your why, you know your strength.

Your why gives meaning to the struggle.

Your why gives purpose to every battle.

Your why brings intention, even to your suffering.

When you know the why to your life, you find the strength to live.

It shouldn't surprise us that when we live in the light, we find our greatest energy. And the contrary is also true. When we live in darkness, we lose our strength. The greatest darkness is to have no meaning for our lives. To live without meaning is to walk in darkness.

Far too much of human history has been written by individuals fueled by the wrong passions. Dictators, tyrants, and despots have marked the human story with destruction and despair. The unwritten backdrop of these stories is that there were endless multitudes powerless to do anything about the violence that overtook them. A careful study of history reminds us that there are often those who had it within their power to end violence, to end injustice, and to end poverty. The painful truth is they simply didn't care enough to act.

Those fueled by greed and hatred will always prevail if their only opposition are those living in apathy and indifference. The great wealth of the world will always be held in the wrong hands if only the greedy are driven to create wealth. Too much of history has been paved by those with destructive intentions. Yet for me, this is not the greatest tragedy of the human story. The great tragedy is the backstory that remains untold. We are simply watching history happen before our very eyes rather than choosing to pay the price to change its course. The future will be created by those who have the courage to create it. A better world will happen only if we find the strength and energy to give our lives to it.

Imagine what would happen if we woke up in the morning energized with hope, consumed by love, and empowered by faith. Imagine the power of those who no longer choose to stand in the middle but instead choose to stand for love against hate, for forgiveness against bitterness, for hope against despair, and for freedom against injustice. Imagine if each person who today is simply lamenting the decay of society would instead gather all their energy and begin to do something to make the world just a little bit better. All evil needs in order to prevail is for good men to do nothing.[72] But if we do nothing, can we by any measure be called good?

Stand Up to Your Pain

The warrior has learned to never underestimate their strength. It is only when you choose the way of the warrior that you discover how strong you actually are and realize there is far more in you than you may ever know. Where once you may have seen pain as the boundary of your limitations, now you know there is a path you can travel if you are willing to walk through your pain.

On the afternoon that I left Huntington Memorial Hospital, approximately eighteen hours after having six hours of surgery to remove cancer, I was finally allowed to go home, but only after being forced to eat at least one meal of hospital food (now, that was almost unbearable pain). Kim drove me home with a concerned entourage of my son, my daughter, and her husband, along with other caring family and friends.

When I got home, it looked as if Kim had prepared our bedroom for me to never leave the house again. She bought a full-sized refrigerator and put it in our room so I could have food and drinks available at all times. She had brought in an electronic chair that turned into a bed with the push of a button so I would never have to move using my own strength. No one expected me to recover quickly or to push myself too hard.

If I have learned one thing in life, it is that if you don't use your strength, you will lose it. There was no comfortable way to escape my limitations. I left the hospital with a catheter, which is a barbaric device used for male humiliation. That by itself would encourage a person to stay hidden in their bedroom. Walking up and down stairs was another real deterrent to my desire to escape the confines of our bedroom.

There had been talk that the catheter would have to remain in for up to a month, and that just seemed unacceptable to me. At my insistence, the catheter was removed after about a week. It's a strange thing to discover a weakness where once you had a strength you previously took for granted. Regaining the strength to control my own body has not lacked a profound sense of humiliation and frustration. The process of regaining my strength—and in fact reclaiming it—has been more textured and layered than I had ever imagined.

About two weeks after my surgery, I called Dr. Khalili, who had performed the surgery and was overseeing my recovery, and asked him what the world's record was for recovering from this surgery and returning to playing basketball. Evidently there was no world's record logged, and that by itself excited me, as I have always wanted to hold one. I cannot overstate how protective my wife and kids have been through my entire recovery. I am surrounded by caring people who worry about the choices I make when it comes to my well-being.

Having been an athlete, I understand the relationship between pain and progress. There is no progress without pain. And if there is no pain, there is no progress. In that regard, you become the boundary of your own freedom. This much is also true of the way of the warrior: progress requires pain and sacrifice. You establish what you can and cannot do. Talent will never be the ultimate cause of your success. You may have unbelievable talent. You may have been genetically endowed with such extraordinary natural abilities that your potential far surpasses everyone else in your field. But it is not talent that determines your limitations; it's tenacity. The warrior's legacy can be written only on the other side of their pain. The way of the warrior teaches us that we cannot stand in our greatness if we cannot stand in our pain.

Rise Above Your Pain

So I set a goal for myself. With six holes in my stomach held together by glue (evidently they don't use stitches anymore), I determined that I would find a way to escape house arrest and run free on a basketball court. The journey began slowly. I decided to embrace my humiliation and began by taking walks in our neighborhood, rolling the catheter right by my side. I made myself take long walks and began going up and down stairs by the second day of my recovery.

Exactly three weeks later (I know this because I wanted to make sure I would always hold the world record), I put all my basketball gear in a sports bag and dropped it down the stairs so that my sweet wife would not see me leave with it. I told Kim that I was going to go out for a while. She looked at me suspiciously right away. "What do you mean you're going out?" I explained to her that I was going to meet some of the guys and get out of the house. I just needed to enjoy the company of good friends. I think right before I left she said something like, "Don't do anything stupid." I don't know why wives waste words like that on their husbands. Of course we're going to do something stupid. It's inherent to our nature.

I drove to a local gym that a few of us had rented just for the occasion. The moment I saw all my guys, I was absolutely energized. I could feel my strength coming back before I threw on my Jordans and held the leather in my hand. We played for two hours that day. Some of the holes in my stomach broke open, and there was some bleeding along the way, but nothing that affected my game. I know it seems like a small thing, but running down that court, stopping on a dime, dropping threes on my much younger, healthier comrades may have saved my life as much as the surgery did.

If you hear nothing else that I'm saying to you, understand this: your freedom is on the other side of your fears. Your greatness lies on the other side of your pain. You will never live the life you were created to live or achieve your greatest dreams if you're not willing to bear the weight of that greatness and pay the price of pain that journey demands.

Other than writing, perhaps the area that has allowed me to do the most good has been speaking. For some reason, I have always been uncomfortable calling myself a preacher. Maybe it's that old-school connotation that you're preaching at people. But I find incredible fulfillment in knowing that you can speak life into people, that words have the power to change people's futures. So I told myself, *You cannot get on a stage to preach until you have the strength to dribble and drive.* Playing basketball is just a pleasure. Speaking life into people—that's my passion.

The reason I share this part of my story with you is so that you will not underestimate your own strength—so that you will know your own power. You may be reading this and feel as if you have lost your spirit, your energy, your will. Yet it's not incidental that the word *encouragement* means to put courage into someone, and the word *inspiration* means to breathe into them. God wants to place both courage and spirit within you. He wants to restore your strength.

Strength in Numbers

Isaiah spoke to people who thought they could not take another step. He brought them encouragement and inspiration: "He gives strength to the weary and increases the power of the weak. Even youths grow tired and weary, and young men stumble and fall; but those who hope in the LORD will renew their strength. They will soar on wings like eagles; they will run and not grow weary, they will walk and not be faint."[73]

Looking back, I realize that the strength I found was not only in the strength that God placed in me but in the strength of the people around me. It was not only the power of the people around me but how their voices informed and formed who I am. Your tribe will shape your identity, and your identity will shape your future. There is something mysterious about the way humans are designed. We are designed to be made strong by the strength of others. We find courage in the courage of others. We are energized and inspired through the energy and inspiration of others. If you're full of inertia and cannot find your way back to strength, then find your way back to people who are strong. Get in an environment filled with optimism and hope. Allow your soul to be nourished by the courage and inspiration of others.

I have the great privilege of meeting and knowing some of the world's most extraordinary people. One of those people is fitness instructor Angela Manuel-Davis. I don't think it's an exaggeration to say that here in Los Angeles, Angela would be considered royalty. Her kingdom is found in a small room in West Hollywood known as SoulCycle, a fitness brand that was introduced to many through Oprah Winfrey. I first met Angela at Mosaic with her husband, Jerome. It was then that I began to learn more about the uniqueness of Angela and Jerome, and also SoulCycle, a force that was sweeping the nation.

It's amazing the kind of influence a leader can have in a room that barely holds sixty people. For sixty minutes, Angela takes the rider on a journey on a bike that never moves. Now, although the bike never goes anywhere, *you* do.

Honestly, to describe that sixty-by-sixty-foot room as a kingdom probably isn't the most accurate description. Having now experienced what happens in that room, I realize that for those who are present, it is a church—or at least a profoundly spiritual experience. For sixty minutes, some of Hollywood's most influential artists and celebrities step into Angela's world and allow her to speak into their lives. She has the ear of the very artists and influencers who have the ear of our culture.

Angela and Jerome kept inviting me to attend, but frankly I was terrified of the idea. Cardio is not my greatest strength. While I try to maintain a high level of fitness, I was not in any way deluded enough to believe I was at the level of conditioning that would be required to survive her class. She kept encouraging me: "You can move at your own pace. Don't worry, it's a really dark room. We'll put you in the back. No one will even see you. It's not a competition."

She said all the right things, but she left out one major detail; she didn't tell me what would *really* happen. She didn't tell me how the energy in the room would overwhelm me—how the level of intensity and determination in that studio would compel me to give my best. She didn't tell me how her words there would speak power-fully into my life. She forgot to mention that whatever amount of power and force I could press into those pedals paled in comparison to how fast everything was turning inside me.

I don't remember what the tipping point was, but I finally took Angela up on her invitation. At first she had us close our eyes and take a few moments to pedal and reflect. We meditated on where we were in our lives and where we wanted to be. We began to still our souls and listen to our inner voices. Then she began to explain that the bike was really a metaphor for life and that how we faced the challenges in front of us was indicative of how we would face the challenges of daily living. She told us that we were not different people in different places, one on a bike and one at work, but rather were the same people everywhere we went. Finally, she commis-sioned us to bring our best into the studio and that if we did that, we'd be training ourselves to bring our best into every other room.

Angela declared with such strength and force and certainty that there was more in us than we knew, that we could overcome the pain we felt. She told us to increase the tension on the bike so we'd have to push ourselves harder. We had to decide, we had to choose; we had to increase the pressure, we had to increase the ten-sion, we had to up the ante, we had to decide what kind of challenge we were willing to face, and we had to decide how much strength we would find within ourselves. All the while, she would just keep shouting, "You are fighting for your freedom! You are fighting for your strength."

It's in moments like these that we find the strength of our wills and test our determination. Every time I wanted to quit (and I wanted to quit so many times in those sixty minutes), Angela's words would help me find the strength I did not know I had. Her direction had everyone in the room moving to the left and then to the right, backward and then forward, all of us in this beautiful syncopation that looked like a work of art. She knew that if we could step into the rhythm of everyone else in the room, we would draw from their strength, we would draw from their energy, and we would draw from their power.

Near the end, when everyone was nearly spent, she told us to fight not only for ourselves but also for others and to think of someone we were carrying, someone we were taking across the line, someone we were fighting for, someone we loved. Then she pressed in even further: "The physical pain you are feeling is just a metaphor. It's just a reminder that the real battle is in a spiritual realm." Somewhere in the midst of that, I think she said something like, "I don't care how you look; I care how you live. This is not about looking good; it's about finding your strength."

In a world driven by external perfection, the warrior chooses a different path. When the warrior looks at their own reflection, they see their soul. They know that both beauty and strength are found only within. They realize that everything on the surface is both temporary and superficial.

You will know your tribe by what they see. If they see only your appearance, they are not your people. When they see your essence, that's your tribe. The warrior cares more about essence than about image. The way of the warrior calls out your inner strength, your inner beauty, and your inner courage.

Frankly, I thought having cancer was hard, but SoulCycle pushed me to the limit. I may have spent as much energy pushing the pedals as I did trying not to lose my lunch. My bike never moved an inch, but I traveled light-years in those moments. I was drenched in sweat, yet I walked out of that room with more energy and strength than I had when I'd walked in. The room carried me. Sixty people I had never met carried me. Angela Davis carried me. It was as if she gave everybody in the room a gift that could not be measured by weight or inches or worth. She gave us herself. She gave us her energy and strength.

Life Source

Have you ever heard someone say, "They really energized the room"? You might think that's a metaphor, but it's actually not. It's an observation rooted in reality. We know that humans can give each other colds and flus. We know that even without human contact, we can pass to each other bacteria and viruses. Yet most of us are unaware that we also transmit to one another what occupies our souls.

Your soul is the conduit of your energy. If your soul is empty, you will consume energy from the world around you. The great danger is that you will see people as something to be consumed and discarded when they no longer energize you. When you are full of life, you become a conduit of life. You will become a source of what is good and beautiful and true. People will naturally draw inspiration from your life. They will see you as a source of hope. If you want to clearly see the world you have created within you, look at the world you have created around you. The warrior takes mastery over their energy and becomes a source of life. The warrior is a life source.

If you are filled with despair, you fill the world with despair; if you are filled with bitterness, you fill the world with bitterness; if you are filled with fear, you fill the world with fear. Additionally, that's all you will ever find. No matter where you go, your world is filled with the same energy and intention that fills you.

In the same way, when the warrior is filled with hope, they fill the world with hope; when they are filled with joy, they fill the world with joy, when they are filled with love, they fill the world with love.

Every human being is both a conduit and consumer of energy. When you are fully alive—when your life is marked by love and joy—you bring energy to the world around you. When you are simply struggling with existence, you consume the energy around you. When I asked Angela from SoulCycle, "What is your purpose?" her response was simple and beautiful: "to inspire, to breathe life into people."

The strength of the warrior is not only for themselves but also for the weak. The warrior knows they are made strong so they might help others find their strength. Jesus once said, "I have come to bring you life and life in abundance."[74] This is our greatest strength. When we are fully alive, we have life to give to the world. When we have more life than we need, when we have life in abundance, we should not be afraid of giving our lives away.

There was once a woman who touched Jesus while he was walking in the middle of a crowd. He stopped and looked around and asked, "Who touched me?"[75] His disciples were perplexed, for he was being touched by an endless number of people. But we are told that Jesus felt power leave him. This is one of the most unaddressed passages on power in the Bible. This woman was marked by a disease and was desperate to find her healing. She believed that Jesus would be the source of that healing.

Unlike the rest of the crowd, who touched Jesus without intention, the woman touched his garment believing that what she needed most could be found in only him. In the simplest of terms, her faith became the conduit of God's power flowing to her. It was such a dramatic exchange of power that Jesus felt it. "Who touched me?" is a strange question when you are being pressed against by a crowd, yet somehow she knew he was referring to her. How could she have known that he was singling her out? She wasn't the only one who touched him, but she was the only one who received his power.

What if God's power is waiting for you and all you have to do is reach out to touch him? What if all the energy you need, all the strength you need, all the power you need is within your reach?

When Jesus came face to face with that restored woman, he did not reprimand her for accessing his power but commended her for her faith and released her to go live in a new peace and freedom she had never known.

This is the paradox that the warrior has come to know. They know they are not the source of their own strength. The fire that burns within the warrior is an eternal fire. The warrior knows their strength because they know their weakness. It was Jesus who said, "Apart from the Father I can do nothing."[76] The warrior understands there is no weakness in this. The warrior has found their strength in their weakness. Jesus spoke to Paul about this: "My power is made perfect in weakness."[77] The way of the warrior is to know that God is our strength. The warrior boasts all the more gladly about their weaknesses so Christ's power may rest on them.[78]

The warrior knows they were created by a God who is Spirit. Though we appear as flesh and blood, every cell in our body is energy. All our energy comes from God. What we do with our energy is up to us.

The ultimate expression of energy is light. The way of the warrior is to choose to be a warrior of light. The warrior never forgets the source of that light. The fire that burns within the warrior is a fire ignited by God. The strength of the warrior is a strength given by God. The power of the warrior is the power poured into them by God. The warrior is light because God is light. The way of the warrior is to choose the path where God himself is both light and life.

The first recorded words spoken by God were "Let there be

light."[79] Light is energy in its purest form. We even speak of motion in its ultimate expression as moving at the speed of light. We now know that the entire universe is a manifestation of energy in an endless number of forms. Imagine the strength we would find if in our weakness we simply reached out, touched God, and received his strength. The ultimate expression of energy is not simply light but life. This is the strength of the warrior, that though they walk through darkness, they have found their strength in both light and life. The warrior stands in the darkness as a warrior of light. The way of the warrior is through the darkness, for they know that in its midst, they will be the light. The warrior must find the courage to face their darkness.

If your darkness is fear, then fear is what you must face.

If your darkness is bitterness, then it is bitterness that you must confront.

If your darkness is greed, then it is greed that you must conquer.

If your darkness is self-doubt, then here you must find your courage.

If your darkness is anger, then it is here that the battle must rage.

If your darkness is despair, then you must stare it down with hope.

If your darkness is hate, you must slay it with love.

You cannot move to the light without facing the darkness.

I was twenty years old when I was encouraged to choose a verse or passage from Scripture that I would make my life verse. I was so new to the faith that very little of the Bible was familiar to me, yet somehow I found the most obscure passage that resonated perfectly with my soul. In the midst of his turmoil and his great disappointment with God, Jeremiah stood in the middle of the fire and declared, "But if I say, 'I will not mention his word or speak any longer in his name,' his words are like a fire shut up in my bones. I am weary of keeping it in; indeed, I cannot."[80]

Your energy will be determined by the fire that burns within you. And when the fire within you burns brightly, so will your life. When your fire has been set by eternity, no moment in time can snuff it out. The warrior never forgets that they are fire.

The Warrior Becomes One with All Things

The warrior becomes one with all things. They understand that it is the darkness that separates; the light brings all things together. When all things began, there was only one. God created man in relationship to himself. God created humanity in relationship to creation. God created man, he created woman, and the man and the woman became one. God is one in three and three in one, and everything he creates is interconnected. The warrior understands that the war is between light and darkness, between connection and disconnection, between oneness and fragmentation. The warrior understands themselves to have been created to be one with God, one with others, and one with creation. The warrior finds themselves when they are connected to all things.

Sometimes to see the whole picture, you must first see the missing pieces. We can understand our need for connectedness only by recognizing where we are disconnected. Our most obvious disconnection is with each other. What we long for most, we fear the most.

We long for intimacy but are afraid of it. Humans are designed for relationships, yet relationships are at the center of our struggles. We know we are made for each other, as our souls suffocate when we lack meaningful relationships. We can see that we were created for connection by the intense consequences of disconnection.

When we are disconnected, we experience isolation and loneliness. If disconnection prevails, it turns to bitterness and disdain. You can see the outcome of disconnection wherever there is hatred, hostility, and violence. We divide by race and color and gender and economic and social status, but in the end these perceived differences are simply symptomatic of the fissures of our disconnection.

One of the powerful insights that Scripture allows us to see is the disconnection between us as a humanity that is symptomatic of our disconnection from God. Human brokenness is not an isolated phenomenon; it is the result of a break between us and God that was never intended to happen.

The account of Cain and Abel gives us an insight into the constructive power of connectedness and the destructive power of being disconnected. Before Cain kills his brother Abel, he severs his relationship with God. His disconnection from his brother was the outgrowth of his disconnection from his Creator. When Adam and Eve broke their relationship with God, it damaged their relationship with each other. And although you may not always see your disconnection from God, you can see the consequences of that distance everywhere.

Our identities are rooted in our connectedness. We know ourselves best when we are known best by others. When we are inter-connected as a people, we do not lose ourselves but in fact find ourselves. Your tribe does not obscure your identity but reveals it. So it is in your relationship with God. As you come to know him, you come to know yourself. As you give yourself completely to him, you come to know yourself most clearly. If you want to find proof that we are created for connectedness with God, look at the fractures and friction between humanity and creation.

Every other species on this planet has an intrinsic connected-ness to creation. Even species that we would consider as least valu-able to the ecosystem continue to prove that they have unique and irreplaceable value. From insects to reptiles, from fish and birds to plants and trees, everything in the created order is interconnected and makes a unique contribution to the vitality of the whole.

It appears we are the only species who can violate the laws of instinct and nature and, in so doing, bring marked devastation to the created world. How is it possible that an endless number of spe-cies living in the ocean can coexist without harming the balance of nature, yet one oil tanker created by man can virtually destroy an entire ecosystem? From my vantage point, every environmentalist in the world should believe in God, as somehow humans have the unexplainable capacity to treat nature in unnatural ways. As twisted as it may seem, humanity's destructive capacity may be one of the strongest evidences of the existence of God. Humans are somehow both a part of nature and stand apart from nature. One of the clear-est indications that humans are different from every other species on this planet is our ability to be out of harmony with creation. There simply is no other species that can create plastic. How is it possible that a species within nature could actually create anything that is not biodegradable? It may be that the best evidence that humanity has a broken relationship with God is that we have a broken relationship with nature.

I am convinced that when God initially set creation in order, he desired that the entire universe be interconnected. He created the universe as a reflection of his character and glory. At the outset of human history, the people experienced complete connectedness to God, complete connectedness to each other, and complete connectedness to creation. When humans severed their relationship with God, they broke not only their relationship with their Creator but also the connectedness of humanity. Likewise, it disconnected us from proper relationship with creation. A significant consequence of the Fall was that the earth would no longer cooperate with the will of man; rather, it would now force us to toil and struggle instead of simply enjoying the benefits of the creation we had been entrusted to steward.

Even in our broken state of being, we still stand intimately interconnected to the created order. We walk within an atmosphere that provides the oxygen we need to live. Every second of our lives, we inhale creation and exhale into creation—our contribution to the creative process. Every time we take a drink of water or stop to eat a meal, we become one with creation. We receive from nature what is necessary for life.

We already have a profound connectedness to creation; we simply may be unaware of it. It is our disconnection that allows us to take without respect, to consume without gratitude, to own without responsibility. We are creators that exist within a creation, and this is extraordinary proof of God.

The warrior understands that they are part of a whole. They know they are most powerful when they are one, when they are undivided and committed to the whole. The warrior knows both that they are part of the entire universe and that the entire universe is a part of them.

The fullness of God dwelled in Jesus. It might be hard to imagine the entire universe existing inside one person, but Jesus experienced even more than that. The Creator of the entire universe dwelled in him! In the beginning the entire universe was designed for life. It is not an exaggeration to say that the universe was created for humanity's fulfillment. The entire creation story is written in such a way that it points to humanity as God's principal creation. Every movement in the creation story leads to God's culminating act of creating humanity in his image and likeness. The universe was not created for God. He did not need it. The universe was created for us. The universe is our context for life.

I have heard many people express that they feel that the entire universe is against them. I would like to take a moment to correct that mentality. The entire universe, as it was created, is for you. If you are at war against God, you will also find yourself at war against people. If you are at war against people, you will also find yourself at war with the universe. The reason the universe is for you is because God is for you.

The warrior understands that everything is connected. You are more than the sum total of your parts. You are connected to the Creator of the universe. The good news is that creation is a part of the package. Every good and perfect gift comes from the Father above. He "does not change like shifting shadows."[81] You are more than you know, so stop underestimating who you are. Who you are does not end at the border of your skin. How you became who you are can be attributed as much to the world around you as the world within you. We spend our entire lives trying to become our own people yet find ourselves disconnected and isolated as the result of our need for autonomy and independence. When we are immature, we convince ourselves that we must become strong enough not to need anyone or anything except ourselves, but we were never created to live like this. When we move toward maturity, we begin to understand the interconnectedness of all things. We were not created to be alone; we are not designed to do life by ourselves.

The warrior finds their uniqueness in their connectedness to all things. The superior warrior does not hold a sword; they become one with it. Your sword is everything in your creative process that becomes an extension of yourself. When you choose a sword, it becomes an expression of your own motion and intention.

You see this expressed with such elegance when you watch the artistry of legendary soccer players Messi and Ronaldo as they run down the field and move the ball with such ease toward the goal. We see it in the stroke of Picasso's brush as both paint and canvas

submit to his will. You see the same phenomenon when five basketball players somehow transform from five individuals into one
united team. For three championships, the Golden State Warriors
have reminded us that there is a synergy that creates a connectedness even in the spaces between them. When describing the challenge of facing the Warriors, LeBron James made clear that it was
an issue of facing not just their superior talent but a superior team
intelligence as well. The Warriors are a reminder to all who love the
sport that not even five great players can beat one great team: their
sixth man is the ball. When you watch them play, it feels as if the
ball has a mind of its own, constantly moving through the space
between the players, somehow always finding the player who is
open and most likely to score.

The first man and first woman were supposed to become one
flesh. How is it possible for two to become one in marriage or for five
to become one on a basketball court or for eleven to become one on
a soccer field? How is it possible for a young boy named Pelé, growing up in poverty in the favelas of Brazil, to become one with the
ball, or for the samurai to wield their swords with such elegance and
ease that it could not be any less than an extension of themselves?

I am convinced that all of us have experienced this phenomenon at least once in our lives—an unexplainable connection to another human being, to a moment, to God. It's usually a moment in
which we found ourselves bigger than ourselves, a moment when
we knew things we should not have known and felt ourselves bigger
than the sum total of our weight.

Years ago I was invited to Germany to speak at a leadership

event. I will never forget the experience. There were approximately five thousand leaders from across the country in a convention center. Because I don't speak German very well, I had to use a translator. I knew that my perspectives on leadership, faith, and culture would seem unorthodox to this particular audience.

In the middle of my talk, I made a statement that I knew would be provocative. When I heard the translator repeat my statement, I somehow knew he had stated the exact opposite of what I had just said. I stopped in the middle of my presentation, looked at the translator, and asked him in front of a live audience, "You just changed what I said, didn't you?"

It would not be an exaggeration to say he looked a bit terrified in the moment. He didn't respond right away, so I asked him again by being more specific. "You didn't agree with what I just said, so you changed it to fit what you believe."

There were five thousand witnesses in the room, so I imagine he felt compelled to be honest and simply responded, "Yes, you are right. I did change it." He was perplexed and asked, "How did you know?" Which of course is a great question, since I'm not fluent in German.

How did I know? I can't fully explain it, but I can tell you this: *communication* comes from the same root word as the word *communion*. If you listen carefully enough, you will hear so much more than words. Although I could not understand exactly what he was saying, I could completely interpret the essence. I knew exactly what he said and exactly what he did not say. My words are my sword, and I don't simply speak them; they are a part of who I am. The translator didn't know that changing the meaning of my words without telling me would be as obvious as trying to take a sword out of a warrior's hand.

Even yesterday while I was working through the final edits of this book, I received a call from my agent, Esther Fedorkevich. She called to tell me that she was flying home and the person sitting next to her on the plane pulled out what happened to be my book *The Last Arrow.* What are the chances of that? What are the chances of two strangers sitting next to each other on a flight and one pulling out a book that both of them had in common?

She decided not to tell the other passenger that she was my agent and instead asked him about the book. He explained that he was a C-suite executive at a massively successful company and had been struggling with thoughts of suicide. He explained that one of his friends gave him the book and that even though he did not believe in God, he knew he needed to find meaning in his life. After he shared his story, she shared with him that she and I knew each other and that she is the very agent who helped make that book happen. She called me to let me know that someone who was contemplating suicide was now searching for meaning and that I had become part of his story.

Either the world is full of random, unexpected coincidences, or there is more going on than meets the eye. I have experienced too much serendipity to believe in accidents. There is simply too much proof to deny that the universe is created with intention, that everything is connected, and that we are part of a larger story. I cannot tell you how many times someone has come up to me and told me they became convinced of the existence of God or the reality of Jesus because of a minor random phrase I happened to use in a talk or book that changed everything for them.

Yesterday I met a young woman who could not have been more than twenty-three years old. She told me that, a few months before, she had created a plan to end her life and had gotten all the necessary supplies. Before she could take action, though, she just happened to bump into someone who happened to invite her to Mosaic. She just happened to walk in one night and hear something that she thought could only have been specifically for her. I can't even begin to describe the joy and connectedness I felt as she explained that she had decided to throw away everything she'd need to carry out her plan. She exchanged death for life, disconnection for connection, darkness for light.

I have lived too long to believe that these things are just coincidence. The warrior leaves nothing to chance and finds rest in their intention. The way of the warrior moves you into the path of interconnection. The path of the warrior is filled with an array of seemingly random and serendipitous moments. The warrior does not strive to create divine moments but feels confident that when they walk in their intention, those moments will come to them. The warrior's courage comes in that even when they stand alone, they know they are never alone. The warrior knows that when they move in their intention, the universe moves in their direction.

Years ago I had the opportunity to visit Tokyo. Of all the cities in the world, Tokyo is certainly among my favorites. The Japanese people express a level of elegance, simplicity, and beauty that has always evoked my admiration. On this occasion, I had the opportunity to speak at an event within walking distance of the Shibuya Station. Because of the cultural and spiritual background of the Japanese people, I had been warned that there would be no openness to the message of Jesus.

My lectures on creativity and spirituality were scheduled for several days. I remember very few things about that experience, but there is one person I will never forget. The event organizers were thrilled that a renowned Japanese artist happened to attend the opening event. It was unexpected since she was not a person of faith, nor did she live within hours of Shibuya itself. Yet every day she returned. Every day she took multiple trains, more than a two-hour journey each way, to attend my lectures.

On the last day of the event, she decided to approach me. I sensed a level of intention and urgency that was both unusual and unexpected. I quickly realized that her unexpected openness to the message of Jesus had little to do with the content of my talks. She explained to me that her brother had recently passed away. The reason she kept returning every day was that I looked just like her brother.

I am pretty certain that I have no Japanese DNA in my blood. Though I have been mistaken in many parts of the world as a native of a variety of countries, this particular comparison came quite unexpectedly. It was strange to hear a well-known Japanese creative tell me that I looked like her brother. One thing I knew for certain was that her experience had little to do with what I looked like and everything to do with what she needed to see. I have often wondered if God knew that for her to see Jesus in me, she needed to see her brother in me first. I do not remember her name, but we will always be connected. Unexplainable phenomena such as these are no longer a surprise to me. I expect to stand in divine intersections. The warrior expects the unexpected. The warrior exists in the transcendent. The warrior moves and expects the universe to move with them.

It seems absurd that Adam and Eve could affect the entire universe with one choice. We have understood how their choice to eat from the tree of the knowledge of good and evil influenced their relationship with God, but I am convinced we have underestimated how it affects humanity's relationship to all creation. God told the man and the woman that if they ate from the tree they would surely die, and since then we have attempted to calculate what consequences that moment would have for the human condition and our relationship to the God who created us.

For far too long we've ignored the implications of the relationship between us and the universe. Even those of us who recognize that our souls groan for redemption have not considered that the universe groans as well. Yet that is exactly what Scripture tells us—that all of creation longs for its redemption and that creation itself has been torn by our actions. Nature's turmoil mirrors our soul's turmoil. Creation's disarray is subject to the condition of the human heart.

It's easy for us to forget that we do not exist within creation but in fact are part of creation. Creation was designed to be connected to our choices. One of the consequences of the Fall, beyond our disconnection with God, is a disconnection with creation. The universe was designed to sustain life. The universe exists for the single purpose of providing what we need to live.

We take for granted the remarkable relationship between what we need to live and how creation is designed to the minute detail to match our needs. We need water, and it is specifically designed to quench our thirst and meet our needs. We need food to satiate our hunger, and both vegetables and fruit happen to grow exactly as needed to sustain life. We need oxygen to breathe, and oddly enough our atmosphere is conveniently made up of a perfect composition that keeps us from suffocating.

Still, it goes deeper than this connection. We do not simply exist in nature; we are part of both nature and the universe. When we are born, we are nearly 80 percent water. When we dive into the ocean, 80 percent of us belongs there. You are literally wet both inside and out. Your mass is made up of approximately 65 percent oxygen. You are more than half the same as the atmosphere around you.

When we breathe, we inhale creation and make it part of us; then we exhale carbon dioxide. We don't identify it as such, but breathing is actually a creative process. We transform what we consume into something distinctly different that we release back into creation. What we release provides life for the very plants that protect the oxygen that gives us life. We are organically part of creation and the creative process. Simply by existing, we create an ebb and flow. We breathe the universe in and release the universe that lives within us to return to the whole. Even the trees consume what we create, and we consume what the forest creates. Our flesh and bone will one day return to dust, and in that sense, we are all bound to the earth and are part of it.

For as long as you have breath and with every beat of your heart, there is an electrical fire igniting within you the life that pumps inside your veins. If there was no fire within you, there would be no life within you. In the same way that you are water and wind, you are also both earth and fire. All creation is within you, is part of you. What you experience in the universe outside of you also exists in the universe within you. The universe literally flows through you.

The boundaries we perceive are largely illusions, or, at best, distortions of reality. The universe has one intention: to create life. The universe within you has one divine intention: to create life. Out of the dust, God created us. Out of his breath, he gave us life. We were made of the universe and made to rule over it.

God established humanity as the agent responsible for the health and well-being of all creation. I am convinced that before our relationship with God was severed, we lived not only in oneness with him and each other but with all creation. This connectedness is central to the way of the warrior. Imagine living in such a relationship not only with God but with creation, where all the universe is leveraged for your success. I love how novelist Paulo Coelho poetically describes how the entire universe conspires on our behalf.[82] He is not wrong. Those who misunderstand this reality attribute a consciousness to the universe that it does not actually have. The universe does not know you, nor choose for or against you, but the Creator of the universe does. He knows you intimately.

The God who created everything, in the truest sense, created nothing for himself. Everything expresses his essence, and everything is designed to give him glory and pleasure, but there is nothing that he ever created because he needed it. God does not need the universe. The universe, though seemingly infinite to us and ever-expanding and immeasurably complex, is still too small for God. In this sense the universe does not exist for God; it exists for us. God didn't create the solar system and the atmosphere on this planet for himself. He doesn't need air to breathe or water to drink; we do.

Could it be any clearer that creation, though created by God, was created for us? And even here we see how God designed everything to be interconnected. The water we drink provides exactly what our bodies need so that we can have not only our thirst quenched but our bodies made whole.

There is a paradox in our relationship with the universe. The universe could exist without us, but we could not exist without the universe. The solar system could exist without us, but we could not exist without this particular solar system. The earth could exist without us, but we could not exist without the earth. The atmosphere could exist without us, but we could not exist without this incredibly specific atmosphere. The water that covers this planet could exist without us, but we could not exist without its water. The oxygen we breathe could exist without us, but we could not exist without this oxygen.

The universe is not dependent on our existence, but we are completely dependent on the universe's existence. If the universe did not fulfill its intention, it would be the end of life as we know it. It is undeniable that the universe is not dependent on us but that we are dependent on the universe. It's a little unnerving when you consider how fragile our existence is in relationship to all of creation.

To make it more personal, the intention of the entire universe points directly to you. Even though you are part of creation and exist within creation, you are God's ultimate and most valued creative act. The entire universe exists so that you might live. Although the entire universe is reflective of the creative essence of God, you have the distinction of being created in the image and likeness of him. Only humanity bears the creative image of its Creator.

You are both within creation and above creation. While humanity seems the most fragile component of the universe, only humans carry within them both the creation and the Creator. Scripture tells us that humanity is God's preeminent creation. He commanded humanity to take dominion and rule over creation. The health of the entire earth was entrusted to the care of this delicate species we call humanity.

When the warrior is one with creation, they see beauty all

around them. When the warrior is one with the universe, they are filled with wonder and awe. When the warrior is one with nature, they find their souls at rest. The warrior honors creation but only worships the Creator. It is dangerous to choose a path that makes you blind to the beauty all around you. The warrior finds themselves often and unexpectedly overwhelmed by the beautiful. Though the warrior has known many battles, they find nothing to be as overwhelming as the beauty that compels them to live. The way of the warrior never loses sight of the elegance, artistry, and exquisiteness that surround them on every step of their journey. The warrior is never overwhelmed by the grandness of the universe but is elevated by it. To know that you are part of the universe is to know that you are connected to something bigger than yourself.

The Bible tells us that all creation declares the glory of God. Although the rest of the world may grow deaf to such declarations, the warrior cannot help but hear them. The warrior looks at creation and is filled with wonder and is moved to worship. The warrior lives in a state of awe. While others look for proof of God, the warrior finds it everywhere. The way of the warrior is a life of worship.

The warrior also understands their stewardship over creation. Creation is a gift from God to humanity and must be treated with honor and respect. We cannot say we respect the Creator if we treat his creation with disrespect. The most skilled warrior has learned never to leave a footprint where they have walked. The warrior seeks to live in harmony with creation. The warrior understands the elegant balance that holds nature together. The warrior can be trusted with creation because they live to honor the Creator.

The ancient poets describe our relationship with God by saying we live and breathe and have our being in him, yet this could easily be the way one would describe our relationship with oxygen.[83] In the same way that a fish can live only in water, so we can live only breathing in this particular atmosphere that God created. The oxygen that exists outside of us brings us life as it seeps through every cell in our bodies. We walk on the earth, yet we are also composed of it. We do not simply exist in creation; we are part of creation. Is it possible that we have underestimated the destructive power of disconnectedness? When nature seems to bend to the will of God and man, we call it a miracle. Is it possible that what we define as a miracle is simply the reestablishing of the proper order of creation?

One with the God of Creation

Elijah lived a life that many would consider to be unbelievable. Almost knowing that we might discount Elijah's story, James tells us that Elijah was a man just like us. With intention, Elijah prayed that it would not rain, and for three and a half years that is exactly what happened.[84]

When we read about a miracle of such an extreme nature, we quickly attribute it to the nature of God. But what if it also has as much to do with the nature of man? What if we are more than we know and in our disconnection with God have become less than we were ever meant to be? What if part of what makes prayer so powerful is that it reestablishes the proper relationship with God, with each other, and with creation. The warrior knows that prayer is their greatest weapon. Prayer is the warrior's sword, and they must learn to wield it well. The warrior knows that prayer is far more than simply speaking to God. The power of prayer comes from hearing from God, and prayer becomes our sword when we speak in concert with him.

After three and a half years, Elijah still found himself in a great conflict with two of Israel's darkest rulers, Ahab and Jezebel. There hadn't been a drop of rain in more than three years and suddenly Elijah told Ahab that he heard the sound of a heavy rain. The skies were clear. There were no clouds to be found anywhere. The land was parched and thirsty. There were children who had no memory of what rain looked like, felt like, or sounded like. Yet Elijah heard the sound of something that had not yet come. It's almost as if creation was speaking to him even as he had spoken to it years before.[85] How strange that Elijah could hear the sound of the heavy rain long before the first drops touched the ground.

I am reminded how Adam and Eve hid in their nakedness because they heard the sound of God walking in the garden. Imagine being able to hear the sound of God walking. For most of us, he is painfully silent. It's hard enough for most of us to hear the voice of God. Imagine living in such intimacy with God that you could identify the sound of his steps.

Elijah climbed to the top of Carmel, bent down to the ground, and put his face between his knees. He commanded his servant to go to the sea, look to the sky, and report what he had found. But when he went and looked, there was nothing there. Yet somehow Elijah was undiscouraged. He sent the servant back six times, and each time, the servant would come back with the same report: that there was nothing there.[86]

I am convinced that most of us would have quit at this point. We would have put more confidence in what was seen than what we heard. I know it sounds absurd, but Elijah was hearing sounds from the future. He was listening to what was yet to come. It was the seventh time when the report changed. On the seventh time, the servant saw a small cloud, a cloud the size of a fist, rising from the sea.

I suppose in most cases the servant would have overlooked the seemingly insignificant sign, but if you look hard enough and keep looking long enough, you will see the first signs of the future being ushered in. That was all the confirmation Elijah needed. And we are told that immediately afterward the sky grew black with clouds, the wind rose, and a heavy rain began to fall.

Even many of us who are believers put stories like this into the category of mythology. What if they are in fact a glimpse into what has been lost? What if miracles look like aberrations because we have accepted the world as it is and not as it should be? What if you're supposed to be able to hear the sound of the coming rain, if only you knew how to listen?

In this moment, we see the layers of the connectedness of the activity of God in human history. Elijah had a soul knowledge, in which he knew before it actually happened. Elijah's servant could not see into the unknown, but he was aware at the first sign. Ahab, whose heart was rebellious against God, came to know only after the rain began to fall. And there were probably masses who never even understood that the drought and the downpour were both connected to the activity of God and who forever remained unaware. The warrior hears the rain before it falls. They hear from God when he speaks; they speak to God and he listens; and together they speak to creation and creation moves toward its intention.

The warrior hears the whisper in the wind. The warrior can also whisper to the wind. The warrior does not move into the future from the present. The warrior moves into the present from the future. The way of the warrior is to hear what cannot be heard, to see what cannot be seen, to know what cannot be known. The way of the warrior cannot be walked with instructions from God; it can be walked only through intimacy with him. The warrior does not know where they are going; they know who they are following. The warrior marks their path not by destination but by Presence.

Speak to the Wind

It was September 22, 2016, and I was giving the closing message of the evening at the Mosaic Conference at the theater in the Ace Hotel in downtown Los Angeles. I have spoken an endless number of messages at a countless number of places, and most of them I would have been hard pressed to remember, but this one I will never forget. That day, I recounted a vision described by Ezekiel as he stood in the Valley of Dry Bones. I spoke on how Ezekiel talked to the wind, how he commanded the four winds to come and move and bring life. He stood at the edge of the Valley of Dry Bones and commanded them to breathe and live. He called the wind from the north, from the south, from the east, and from the west and told dry bones to live.[87]

I remember declaring that we are the descendants of those who spoke to the wind and the wind had to bend to their wills—that when we hear the voice of the one who created us and embrace his intention for us, it is then that we discover the power of our own voices and how prayer is more than an exercise in futility. We have the power to speak to the wind. After all, if the Creator of the universe would act on our behalf, how in the world can his creation ignore us?

The strangest thing happened that night. As more than a thousand people exited the building, Los Angeles was suddenly hit with an unexpected and uncharacteristic windstorm. The wind blew with such force that the electricity went out in the area where we lived. We had a small gathering planned for that evening at our house, where the leaders who came from around the world would join us. It was surreal to stand together in a pitch-black room with the wind howling all around us. No one needed to say anything. It was almost as if God extended the message. Years after that evening had come to an end, I am still convinced that the timing was not incidental, that God was speaking through creation, that he was confirming there is more power in us than we know.

A beautiful symmetry that connects all this together is that the same Hebrew word for "wind" is also the word for "spirit" and for "breath." The same is true in Greek. In the Hebrew Scriptures the word is *ruach,* and in the Greek it's the word *pneuma,* which also carries all three meanings in the one word. The same word that describes the breath that gives us life also describes the wind that blows around us. It also describes the Spirit of God, who comes to dwell within us.

So if you are wondering if we can really speak to the wind, I can tell you without question that the breath of God, the Spirit of God, the wind of God, dwells within you. We are a people of the wind, and that wind that is God's Spirit gives us the breath of life, the power of the wind, and the voice of the Spirit.

When Jesus first appeared to his disciples after his resurrection and they were terrified and filled with fear at his appearance, he said to them, "Peace be with you!"[88] And then John described a very unusual detail. He said, "With that he breathed on them and said, 'Receive the Holy Spirit.'"[89]

It is more than incidental that John noticed that Jesus breathed on them as he told them to receive his Spirit. Remember, the same word for "spirit" is the same word for "wind" and the same word for "breath." We live because the breath of God is within us. His breath is the wind of his Spirit. This imagery takes us back to the moment

God created the first man. With everything else in creation, he simply declared it into existence. He proclaimed, "Let there be light,"[90] and the light came into existence. He spoke, and the universe was created.

But with man it was different. After God formed the man out of the dust of the ground, he "breathed into his nostrils the breath of life, and the man became a living being."[91] The man came to life when he breathed deeply of God. Jesus, when he breathed on his disciples, was restoring this intimate and profound connection. It should not surprise us that a short time later when God's Spirit poured out on his people, Luke could describe it only as the sound of a rushing wind. Can we still speak to the wind? Only if we can hear it speaking to us.

To See the Wind

When Jesus walked among us, he spoke to the waves and to the wind and commanded them to be still, and they became silent. We often refer to this as proof that Jesus was fully God. But is it possible that this was a window into another truth—that Jesus was fully human? It makes sense that we would attribute everything that Jesus did, that we cannot do, to his divinity. The implications are too great for us to bear if they are actually also expressions of his humanity. So much of what Jesus came to do was not simply to point us back to God but to reflect to us what it means to be created in the image of God.

None of us who have come to know Jesus as the Son of God

would be surprised by the fact that he walked on water. Of course Jesus could walk on water: he is the God who created the water. This would be nothing for God, but no small thing for us. Yet on that occasion when Jesus walked on the water to meet his disciples while they worked their way across the sea, it was Peter who once again asked for the outlandish: "Jesus, tell me to come to you."[92]

It's almost as if Peter understood that if God spoke to him and told him to walk on the water, the water would have to bend to his will. Jesus simply tells him to come, and Peter steps out of the boat and walks on the water, even if for only a moment, for a step or maybe two.

Do you understand the implications of this moment? I must confess that I have no idea what the limits of human capacity may be when we actually begin to live out the fullness of the image of God as we walk in his intention for us. What I do know is that far too many of us have surrendered ourselves to being less than God's intention for us. I also know that it will take an act of faith for us to become more.

Strangely, we are told that Peter began to sink when he saw the wind and it terrified him. I find it curious that many translators actually augment what Scripture specifically says and replace the word *wind* with *waves,* or at the very least try to explain it away.[93] The Bible does not tell us that Peter saw the *waves;* it tells us that he saw the *wind.* We reinterpret it because our experience tells us that you can see waves but not wind—unless, of course, you are walking on water. Maybe if you are walking on water you can see wind.

As far as I know, walking on water hasn't happened since Jesus and Peter did it. And maybe in terms of our present history, that was a unique phenomenon for a specific moment in time. What I do know is that there are places God wants to take you that are beyond your own capacity. What I am certain of is that the journey of faith always feels like walking on water and seeing the wind.

Even while I write these words, my wife is walking among the villagers in Lilongwe, Malawi, with a team of thirty-four other people. They have left the comfort of their own homes and the safety of their own country to go where they would not have journeyed if God had not called them. What you need to think about when you recall Peter walking on water is not that you should be intent on walking on water as well but that you need to see where Jesus is and hear where he is calling and go there regardless of what you have to walk through. You must walk with confidence, knowing that neither water nor wind can keep you from God's intention in your life and that in fact the universe will pave the way for you if you will decide to walk forward.

So my question to you is simply this: What boat do you need to get out of? That is, what's the next step you must take? We all have more than enough excuses to stay in the boat and more than enough reasons to explain why we could never walk on water. By the way, you might be well aware that eventually Peter began to drown. That's not the unexpected part. You should expect that this would be a real possibility if you venture to walk on water.

When Peter began to be enveloped by the waves, he cried out to Jesus and asked him to save him. It's comforting to know that Jesus immediately reached out and pulled him out of the waters. He pulled Peter back to his feet, and while they were both standing on the water, Jesus had a brief conversation with Peter about his lack of faith. Then after capitalizing on what must have been an impressive teachable moment, Jesus walked with Peter back to the boat.

The walk back, from my perspective, is far more profound than the steps Peter took to get to Jesus. You would think that after Peter began to drown he would have to be carried back by Jesus or maybe even swim by Jesus's side while Jesus walked back on the water alone. Instead, Peter was able to accomplish, after he began to drown in his doubt, what he could not do before his moment of failure. Peter's entire perspective of what was possible had to have been dramatically changed in that moment.

Jesus prayed that we all would become one as he and the Father are one.[94] I don't think we have even begun to comprehend the implications behind that prayer. We are so conditioned to living disconnected from everyone else and everything else that the concept of oneness eludes us. What kind of creatures can hear the rain before it comes and see the wind when it blows and walk on water when God says to come? What kind of creatures can hear the sound of God walking in the garden in the cool of the day? Who can commune with God while thrown into a fiery furnace and still escape unburned? It would seem that only angels could hear God whisper when they are hiding in a cave or see in a dream the future that awaits. Yet in each of these cases, we find it is the story of God and man walking together in time and space.

Maybe we have underestimated what it means to be human. Is it possible that the stories preserved for us in Scripture are not simply there to inspire us but to provoke us? After all, Elijah was a human being, just as we are,[95] and more importantly, he was *just* a human. Then why doesn't our humanity reflect this kind of experience, this kind of life?

When you become one with God, you begin the journey to become one with others, and to your surprise, you will also find that you become one with the universe around you. Jesus is the intersection of all things. It is Jesus who dwells in perfect union with God and man and creation. To become one with all things, you must first become one with Christ. Jesus came to reconcile all things. He came to reconcile us to God, to reconcile us to one another, and to reconcile us to creation.

In fact, the Bible tells us that all creation groans for its redemption. We couldn't see it, but when we severed our relationship with God, we created a tear in the universe. Ironically, the universe seems more aware of its brokenness than we are of ours. Yet the groaning of the universe is only an echo of the groaning within the heart of humanity. The universe within you has a tear, and it groans for its redemption. Only Jesus can heal that tear and redeem you to life.

The Creator of the universe stepped into his creation, became like one of us, and gave his life so we could live. He allowed himself to be broken so he might heal our brokenness. The cross is the intersection of all things. We know this about Jesus:

The Son is the image of the invisible God, the firstborn over all creation. For in him all things were created: things in heaven and on earth, visible and invisible, whether thrones or powers or rulers or authorities; all things have been created through him and for him. He is before all things, and in him all things hold together. And he is the head of the body, the church; he is the beginning and the firstborn from among the dead, so that in everything he might have the supremacy. For God was pleased to have all his fullness dwell in him, and through him to reconcile to himself all things, whether things on earth or things in heaven, by making peace through his blood, shed on the cross.[96]

Not only was everything created through God and for God, but only in Jesus do all things hold together. It is because of this that only through him and through his sacrifice on the cross are all things reconciled to himself. It is through him that the separation that defines our existence can be finally overcome. This then becomes our imperative: to reconcile the world. The warrior knows that peace can come only through reconciliation. When the warrior is one with all things, they are at peace with themselves.

As it says in Hebrews, "Without faith it is impossible to please God."[97] I have always thought that was an unfair expectation placed on humanity that God holds no other species accountable for. We are the only species in all creation that cannot please God without faith. Salmon fight to swim upstream, to lay their eggs, and while it is a great battle, there is no faith involved. The eaglet must one day be pushed out of the nest by its mother in hopes that its wings are strong enough for it to sustain flight, but faith is not required. A fish may have to share an ocean with a shark, but God never holds it accountable for its faith.

Why is it that only humans are held to this standard? Why is it that without faith we cannot please God? The reason is both simple and significant: we are the only species in creation that can live beneath its intention. Everything in creation is created with intention, as everything in creation reflects the intention of God. Whether it is wheat or weeds, bees or butterflies, wolves or antelopes, everything in creation has its place, its relationships, and its intention. We have seen in our own lifetimes how returning wolves to their natural habitat radically restores a crippled ecological system.

In the most elegant complexity possible, everything in creation exists not for itself but for everything interconnected to it. It's hard to conceive that the blue whale, the sea's giant, lives on nothing more than the ocean's plankton, which is hardly perceivable by the human eye. It's perplexing that humanity is the one species with awareness and is simultaneously so unaware of creation's dependence on its choices. We are the one species that holds creation hostage, yet we are as dependent on nature as it is on us. I note this only to make us aware of a greater reality: that although a tiger is always a tiger and a cobra is always a cobra, neither can do anything outside its intention.

Yet humans can live inhumane lives. Humans can live beneath their intention. Humans can violate the essence of who they were created to be. Even those who do not believe in the Creator or that we were created in his image find themselves perplexed by their own language. We never judge the morality of a tiger or cobra. We never conclude that a scorpion or black widow has violated some code of ethics or has chosen to live a life beneath their intention. However, humans can create or do things that we would define as unnatural and can commit heinous crimes against one another. Such actions are called inhumane.

Yet God's intention for you exceeds this. For some, the language of faith seems to imply that we will live lives that are *super-human*. What I have come to know, and what Scripture reveals, is that faith actually makes us human again.

Being Human

The reason we cannot please God without faith is that faith restores our humanity. We were never designed to operate outside of faith. When we live without faith, we lose our proper relationships with God, with each other, and with the universe. In the same narrative, we are told that faith moves us toward confidence in what we hope for and assurance in what we do not see.[98]

This description contradicts the whole of human experience. It is most natural to have more confidence in what you actually have than what you hope for. What you have exists in the present, but what you hope for exists only in the future. When your hope is in the past, you are hopeless.

So faith causes a shift inside a human spirit. It moves the warrior from confidence in what they have to confidence in what they hope for. It moves us from being creatures trapped in the past or contained by the present to being intimately connected to the future. Jackals don't have futures; they only have the present. Elephants may have great memories, but they have no perception of the future. The human species is the only one aware of the future and in fact capable of creating it.

Faith not only shifts our confidence from the present to the future but also from the realm of the visible to that of the invisible. Faith is not only confidence in what we hope for but assurance in what we do not see. This does not coincide with natural human experience. Left to ourselves, we have assurance in only what we do see, or at the very least we have far more assurance in what we see than what we don't. Right in the heart of the United States sits Missouri, whose very nickname is the Show-Me State. I don't think we have a state whose central tenet is "See the invisible."

The way of the warrior is a journey into the future invisible. The warrior understands that they must not fight for the past but fight for the future, that their weapons are not the weapons of this world but are divinely powerful and unperceivable by the natural man.

The author of Hebrews reminds us that "by faith we understand that the universe was formed at God's command, so that what is seen was not made out of what was visible."[99] The writer used creation as the example to help us understand how we are to live because we are creation. God made everything that is visible out of what is invisible, and all that is visible and invisible is subject to his command.

This is what it means to live by faith. This is not a new way but an old one. The ancients were commended for this life of faith. Faith is connectedness to the future and to the invisible. It is connectedness to the transcendent and the eternal. This is how we were intended to exist. This is how life was meant to be lived. When we stand in our intention, we are the ones who walk on water, who command the four winds to breathe into dead bones. We are the ones who call down fire from the heavens. We are the ones who stand before the sea and tell the waters to part and make a way.

I was new in my journey of faith. I didn't know much about God or the Scriptures or the way of the warrior. All I knew is that I had come to know the Creator of the universe and that his name was Jesus. My instructions about faith were fairly limited. I was told to read the Bible and meditate on its truth, to pray with the expectation that God would hear me, to listen with the expectation that God would speak. I was also told that the same God who wrote Scripture is the very God who would write the pages of my story as well.

I was only twenty years old and a student at Elon University, and I quickly began to meet other people of faith. There was one person in particular who had a dramatic effect on my early pilgrimage. She was young and vibrant and from all appearances seemed to have a dynamic and unshakable faith. Yet one day she confided to me that before coming to the university, she had lived a very different life. She had been living with a former boyfriend, and they were heavily involved in some self-destructive patterns. Unexpectedly, she expressed to me that she had recently contacted him and decided to return to her former way of life.

At that point in my faith journey, I couldn't imagine why anyone would choose to walk away from God once they had come to know him, but I could see she was in pain. I asked her where she felt God was in all of this, and she confessed that God no longer seemed real to her. I wasn't trained for this. Faith was still new to me. I just knew that God would not give up on her even if she had given up on him.

Maybe it was my own sense of desperation, but I said to her, "If there's anything God could do to prove his love for you, I know he would do it." I understand now that probably wasn't the wisest thing in the world to say, but it's what came to mind in that moment. I don't know what I expected her to say. I hadn't thought enough ahead to try to predict her response.

She looked at me and said, "Well then, if God loves me, I want him to make it snow." Now, it's not that it doesn't snow in North Carolina, but on that day there was no expectation of snow. Zero possibility of snow. No precipitation in sight. It was suddenly for me a gloomy clear day.

As troubling as her request was, my response was even more disturbing. I really can't tell you why I said what I said. All I know is that without hesitation, I looked at her and told her, "God is going to make it snow to prove to you that he loves you."

I know now that the ultimate proof of God's love is that he sent his Son Jesus to die on the cross in our behalf. It's just not what came to my mind right then. The very moment I heard myself say it, I wanted to give myself a little time. But because I was in panic mode, instead of saying that God might need more than twenty-four hours, I told her it would definitely happen within twenty-four hours. I don't remember any of the conversation after that. I just went back to my dorm room, closed the door, pulled down the shades, turned off the lights, fell on the floor, and began to pray.

I wasn't completely sure what had just happened. Did God speak to me and I simply echoed his words? Or did I overstep my boundaries and make a promise I could not keep? So as I prayed, I tried to cover all my bases: *God, if that wasn't you, could you make it happen anyway? I'm new at this. I have been on this path for only three months. I'm still trying to find my way.*

But what I believed happened was that God spoke to me, that I heard his voice, that he told me to speak to the creation and declare its intention. And that's exactly how I said it to her. I declared that it would happen. I was standing on the water. Now I was looking at the wind. And maybe as I prayed with uncertainty, I too found myself drowning under the force of the waves.

And then I fell asleep. And while I was praying and sleeping, I didn't know what my friend was doing. Apparently, she was telling every person she saw that God was going to make it snow for her because he loved her. It's amazing how fast a story like that will spread across a university campus.

It wasn't more than an hour later that my roommate walked into our room and disrupted my sleep—I mean prayers. He didn't say hello or ask me how I was doing. He just simply looked at me and asked, "Have you looked outside?"

I remember getting up and walking cautiously to the window, taking a deep breath, and pulling up that ugly yellow shade. I thought he was asking that question to mock me, to let me know I had lost all my credibility, but that was not the case at all. When the shade cleared the window, I couldn't believe my eyes. There was snow everywhere. It clearly had been snowing almost from the moment I had hidden myself away, afraid of what I had done.[100]

You can try to explain this any way you want, and if you find it hard to believe, so do I and I was there. But that moment became a part of my history nearly forty years ago, and I have never been the same since. I have been listening to the voice of Jesus calling me to where I clearly cannot go without him.

Some want to treat Peter's walking on the water and seeing the wind as only a metaphor. This is a massive disservice to that account. We need to allow the truth of his story to dismantle our views of reality and open us to the endless possibilities of what God can do with us in this life.

I know that God still speaks. He still does the impossible. He still calls us to lives that can be lived only by faith. Can we really walk on water? Can we really call down fire from heaven? All I know is that on one particular day, I heard a voice telling me to declare to the universe that the snow would come—and it did. All I can really speak to is that at least for a moment, I was connected to all things and heard the snow before it fell, and I cannot live with any lesser truth than this.

The Eternal One

Enoch was taken from this life so that he would not experience death. He could not be found on the earth because God had taken him away. Before he was taken, he was commended as one who pleased God. Scripture summarizes his life this way: "Enoch walked faithfully with God; then he was no more."[101] We tend to see life and death as linear and sequential. This might be why we see time and eternity in the same way. The warrior knows that eternity does not wait on time. For the warrior, eternity is now, and now is eternity. The warrior walks in the eternal because they walk in oneness with God.

Abraham looked forward to a city that had not yet been built; Joseph lived through years of imprisonment knowing that his dreams were windows into the future; Noah built an ark before the world had ever known rain. Each of them lived as if they were time travelers coming from the future and preparing us for what was yet to come.

The warrior does not live in the past, nor are they ever trapped in the present. While their life may seem extraordinary, all they have done is reclaim their humanity. They understand that their strength is not formed in standing alone but in connectedness to all things. They see God everywhere and always moving. They see his fingerprints in every page of human history. They feel him moving in the wind, hear his roar in the ocean, and know his presence in every breath.

Some find it hard to see God anywhere. The warrior finds it impossible not to see him everywhere. Everything is connected. This is your power; this is your strength—that you're never alone. You are one with God and with all of his creation.

Solomon wrote in the book of Ecclesiastes that God has "set eternity in the human heart."[102] The implications of this verse reach far beyond everything we've considered so far in this chapter. Though you are part of creation and were created to be connected to all things, you are most profoundly connected not to time, not to space, but to eternity. This is what makes humanity different from every other creation in the created order. Even while you are bound in time and space, you cannot be contained by it. You belong to eternity.

Jesus said, "Whatever you bind on earth will be bound in heaven, and whatever you loose on earth will be loosed in heaven."[103] The implications of this verse and the verse in Ecclesiastes are so powerful that they may actually reach beyond our comprehension. The connectedness that we are called to goes beyond what is visible to the invisible, beyond the created to the eternal, beyond the finite to the infinite.

The warrior does not belong in time, for the soul of the warrior is timeless. The warrior is both fully present in the moment and fully present in the eternal. The warrior sees the eternal in every moment, the infinite in every detail. The warrior knows they can know heaven on earth, and, more importantly, they can bring heaven to earth. The way of the warrior is the end of separation. The warrior is one with all things.

The Warrior Stands in Their Pain

The warrior bears their wounds well. Their scars carry a beauty that only sacrifice can create. The warrior never hides their scars. They know their scars are the story of their life. The one who has no wounds has never fought a battle. The warrior trusts only the person who bears wounds openly and wears them well. Some wounds are so deep that they take years to heal; other wounds are unseen, and the healing takes a lifetime. The warrior knows that the battle will cause them great pain, anguish, and suffering. You do not go to war because you think you can avoid defeat. You do not go to war because you believe that victory is certain. You go to war because you know you must fight.

I do not want you to lose the intent of my teachings. You must never forget that the warrior fights only for peace. And while we will always live in a world of war and rumors of war, the warrior has a single intention: to win the battle raging within. If you are intent on studying your adversary and securing your victory, you must know yourself. You must know that the battle is within. This is the battle I seek to help you win. The world has always been at war, and if left to its own devices, war will be not only our history but our destiny.

The pages of this book carry one clear intention: to win the battle for peace one person at a time, one heart at a time, one soul at a time. You cannot bring peace to the world if you have never come to know peace within yourself. And strangely enough, even if you have been given the luxury of living in a time of peace or in a place on this earth that is untouched by war, your soul will not know such luxury. The peace you long for will come only when you choose to face your greatest battles. If you run from your fears, you will never conquer them. If you run from your pain, you will never be free of it. If you run from the darkness within, you will never become a warrior of light, which is both your intention and your destiny. Your wounds do not disqualify you from taking the warrior's path. It would be fair to say that the warrior is more familiar with pain than the one who has surrendered to a lesser intention.

The warrior stands in their pain. Their wounds are their badge of honor. Every battle is first fought within. Every victory secured for your future is first fought for in your struggle for faith. To live in the light, you must first face your inner darkness. Your external battles are won or lost in your inner world. You cannot separate world peace from inner peace. You cannot separate the daily battles you will face from the unseen battles that seem faceless.

Even in the midst of writing these chapters, I faced a crossroads in which I had to decide whether to stand or withdraw. I had been invited to speak at a significant event. What once seemed an unprecedented opportunity now carried the weight of unimaginable controversy and pain. Without going into detail, I felt the social and even global weight of responsibility of whether I should withdraw from speaking at the event or honor my commitment. Multiple speakers chose to cancel, and I understood their reasoning, or at least their decision. But as I prayed, I heard such a clear voice speak to the depth of my soul. As clearly as I heard the opening words of this book, "The warrior is not ready for battle until they have come to know peace," I heard these words: "The warrior stands where others withdraw."

I went and I stood in the midst of people who were carrying great pain. They had been wounded and even betrayed by the leaders in whom they had put their trust. One person deeply affected by the controversies and wounds that surrounded them expressed to me, "I thought leaders ran into the fire and not away from it."

If you choose the way of the warrior, you will bear many wounds. Yet the wounds you will bear will not end with your own. The warrior bears the wounds of others. The warrior bears the wounds of the world. The warrior knows the only wounds that can heal are the ones they are willing to bear within them.

In victory every warrior looks to be brave and courageous. Yet it is defeat that strips you bare and forces you to see your truest self. Success allows you to maintain the illusion of who you are. It is in failure that you come to know yourself best. The skills of a warrior may help them in victory, but they are useless to them in defeat. When you face defeat, all you're left with is yourself. It is then that you will face your greatest battle. You will find yourself at war with the darkness within. Your greatest danger will be to convince yourself that you are beyond the reach of this darkness, that you have traveled so far that your soul is impenetrable. Yet the warrior learns that their greatest victories and defeats often come like two sides of the same sword.

The battles we fight become inescapably both internal and external. Victory in one battle does not secure for us victory in another. You may be winning the battle within to live your most heroic and courageous life and yet still lose your job and find yourself in financial peril. You can in the same moment that you achieved the pinnacle of success in your career come home to face the end of your marriage. We've seen through the tragic loss of extraordinary talents such as Anthony Bourdain and Kate Spade that the victories on the outside may only be hiding the battles lost within. All of us are portraits of contradiction. In those moments we feel most indomitable, we find ourselves most fragile.

Fire and Ashes

The prophet Elijah once stood alone against nearly a thousand false prophets. With a multitude of onlookers, he challenged the false prophets to a battle to prove the power of the gods they worshiped. The battle was to be conducted with some unexpected weapons and circumstances. Both Elijah and the false prophets would build an altar and prepare an offering to their gods, yet they would not light an actual fire as they would typically do in order for the animal sacrifices to be consumed. Elijah set the terms of the challenge: the false prophets would pray to their god and ask for fire to come down from heaven and consume the altar. Then Elijah would pray to his God and make the same request.[104]

Elijah and the false prophets agreed to the terms, and the battle began. The measure of success would be simple: the deity who answers by fire is the true God. All of the bystanders understood the scenario and what was at stake. Elijah put his entire reputation and the reputation of God on the preposterous notion that God would send this fire from heaven.

The prophets of Baal cried out to their god from morning until noon, but there was no response. They danced and danced to get his attention to no avail. They shouted louder and louder, but Baal was silent. And then, as was the custom of their dark religion, Baal's prophets began cutting themselves with swords and spears until their blood flowed as an offering to their god. But nothing they could do could make a god who did not exist answer their prayers. As the evening came, their frantic attempts to awaken Baal ended in utter futility. No one responded. No one answered. No one paid attention.

It should be noted that Elijah was not merely sitting by during this time. Scripture indicates that he taunted the prophets of Baal and encouraged them to shout louder and made fun of the apathy and inactivity of their god. "Perhaps he is in deep thought," he proposed, "or busy, or traveling. Maybe he is sleeping and must be awakened."[105] Elijah was determined to leave no ambiguity or uncertainty about who was the one true living God.

When the prophets of Baal conceded their failure, Elijah stepped up and called the people to come close to him. He went above and beyond the initial terms of the challenge. He dug a large trench around the altar and instructed the people to fill four large jars of water. He had them pour those jugs of water on the offering and the wood. Then he told them to do it again, and then he ordered them to do it a third time. They must have thought Elijah was out of his mind. Wasn't it hard enough to pray fire down from heaven without having to water down the altar?

The altar was drenched with water running down, even filling the trench built around it. Then Elijah stepped forward and prayed. He asked God to make his presence known and to help his people turn their hearts back to him again. Without hesitation, without a lapse of any notable time, a fire fell from heaven; burned the sacrifice, the wood, the stones, and the soil; and also consumed all the water in the trench. When the people saw this, they fell to their faces and cried out, "The LORD—he is God! The LORD—he is God!"[106]

Even as observers, we revel in moments of great victory. When Brazil wins a World Cup, an entire nation dances in the streets. This was Elijah's pinnacle moment. This was the Red Sox beating the Yankees, the Cavaliers beating the Warriors, the Eagles beating the

Patriots. In moments like these, you feel invincible. The problem, of course, is that you are not.

After an experience like this, you would think that Elijah was untouchable, that his resilience was impenetrable, and that nothing could ever shake his faith or cause him to be discouraged or afraid. Yet surprisingly we find that the very opposite was the case. After this defining moment in Elijah's life, in which the presence and power of God was undeniable, Elijah was actually most vulnerable to the frailness of his humanity. How did Elijah go from victoriously calling down fire from heaven to mourning and covering himself in ashes?

When Ahab and Jezebel heard what Elijah had done, Jezebel sent a message to Elijah to let him know that by the same time the next day, she would make certain that his life would come to an end.[107] What I would expect from Elijah would be for him to send a message back to Jezebel, something like "Who do you think that you are? And who do you think I am?" After all, calling fire down from heaven should create a significant amount of self-confidence.

But instead, "Elijah was afraid and ran for his life."[108] This seems to me an extreme response after such an extraordinary victory—except when I look at my own life. So many times I have found myself most vulnerable after I had seemed most unstoppable. Those who see you from a distance will notice the battles you fight for them but not the ones you fight for yourself. Most wouldn't have predicted that Elijah would be afraid and run. Although it is true that success breeds success and courage fuels courage, it is also equally true that every warrior of light has to fight against their own darkness.

It's no small irony that in response to his fear, Elijah ran for his life. The truth is, he didn't run for his life; he ran *from* his life. Unexpectedly, the last victory did not leave him with the strength for the next battle. This is one of the reasons it's so important to celebrate every victory and make sure you take the time to replenish your strength. After all, the reward of winning a great battle is a greater battle. Sometimes this feels like more than we can bear.

There are moments even for the greatest of warriors in which we just don't know if we have the strength to carry our weapons once more into battle. Sometimes the weapon is faith, at other times the weapon we need most is hope, and of course our most powerful weapon is love. When we are full of fear, faith can feel too heavy to lift. When we are drowning in despair, hope can feel more like self-delusion. If we allow hate to seep into our souls, love feels less like a weapon in our hands and more like an anchor around our neck. The warrior knows that their only weapons are faith, hope, and love. Only these will carry us through the battle. Only faith, hope, and love can give us the peace we seek and create the peace the world so desperately needs.

The Dark Side of Victory

I have tried to live a courageous life, even a heroic life. I have attempted wherever possible to make decisions that reflect my faith. But I can tell you that there have been many times when all I have wanted to do is run and hide. The paradox is that outside observers would have been certain I was having the time of my life. All they could see is one battle won after another. Just because someone's life can be mapped through a series of great victories doesn't mean they have been exempted from the struggles we all face from within.

Elijah had great faith and great courage, yet in this moment when he fled from Jezebel, we find him drowning in fear and doubt. Elijah is a poignant reminder that even when we have faith, we are vulnerable to fear—that even when we have hope, we are still susceptible to despair. The warrior knows that the light and the darkness are at war within them. No matter how they look, every hero is still human. Elijah was no different. The warrior knows their strength, and, perhaps more critically, they know their weakness. Elijah went from standing with an unwavering faith against insurmountable odds to running for his life and being overtaken by an irrational fear.

After he was too exhausted to run any farther, he came to a broom bush and sat under it. What kind of prayer would you expect a man like Elijah to pray in a moment like this? *Lord, in the same way that you brought fire down from heaven and in the same way you closed the heavens and withheld rain, I am asking you to take care of Ahab and Jezebel.* That's the prayer I would expect. *God, you have already demonstrated your power. You've already made it undeniable that you are with me. Just tell me where to go and what to do, and I'm there.* That's what I could anticipate him saying. But in actuality his prayer was quite the opposite.

He sat down under the bush and prayed that he might die. " 'I have had enough, LORD,' he said. 'Take my life; I am no better than my ancestors.' Then he lay down under the bush and fell asleep."[109] It seems to me the only hope Elijah had was that God would end his life in the quietness of his slumber. I don't think he expected to awaken to the same life from which he had run.

One of the most perplexing realities I have had to learn is that in the wake of my greatest victories will come crashing into my soul my greatest despairs. They will be commensurate to their statuses: the greater the heights of victory, the greater the depths of despair. Don't let anyone ever tell you that fear makes you a coward. The moment you believe you are not vulnerable to the most basic of human frailties, you have postured yourself to be shattered to pieces. Everyone gets discouraged. And by its very etymology, to be discouraged is to lose your courage. More of us than will ever admit will struggle with depression or being depressed. Life carries great weight, and if you find the courage to take on great battles, you will feel an even greater weight that will sometimes seem more than you can bear.

I am a person who loves life and continuously pursues living fully, but I fully identified with Elijah's prayer: "I have had enough, Lord. Take my life." I wish I could tell you that I have never known this kind of darkness, but I have. I wish I could tell you that as filled with hope as I have been on my journey, I have never felt myself suffocating under an overwhelming sense of despair, but I have never been exempt from those struggles. I have known them all too well. There are days I cannot sleep because of worry, and others when I don't want to wake up to face the battles that I know are coming. I have had too many people I have loved come to the end of themselves, and too many who have chosen to end themselves, to treat this moment in Elijah's life lightly.

Elijah the prophet of God wanted God to end his life, and we should pause and reflect deeply about this truth. The warrior is not free from the darkness but must face darkness and bring to it the light.

When Life Is More Than You Can Bear

I am profoundly moved by God's response to Elijah's fragile and frail condition. I think if Elijah were alive today and responded in the same way, he would be the target of antagonism, judgment, and condemnation. He would be seen as unworthy of leadership. He would be told to stop focusing on himself and to put his focus back on God. He would be judged for his lack of faith, condemned for succumbing to his depression, and ridiculed for running away and not facing the realities of life.

God instead responded with incredible gentleness and compassion. An angel was sent to touch Elijah and instruct him to get up immediately. No loud noises, no angry rebuke or reprimand, no condemnation for his cowardice—just a simple caress to wake him from his sleep and encouragement to get up and eat.

Startled by this intervention and unaware that food was available, Elijah quickly looked around. By his head there were freshly baked bread and a cool jar of water. After Elijah ate and drank, he lay down again. Have you ever noticed that when you are depressed, all you want to do is sleep? You may not even have the strength to eat or drink, but if someone brings you a food or beverage, you'll submit to their offer and then go back to sleep. This is exactly what Elijah did.

But the angel of the Lord came back a second time and gently touched him again. This time the angel added a bit more information to his encouragement: "Get up and eat, for the journey is too much for you."[110] I don't think it's incidental that on his first appearance, the angel didn't mention the journey ahead; he just told Elijah to get up and eat. The second time the angel appeared, he began to speak to Elijah about his future. He didn't say that things were going to get easier. He didn't say not to despair because there weren't any challenges ahead. He spoke the truth: *Elijah, you need to regain your strength because the journey ahead is too much for you in your present state.* The warrior knows that the strength they have today won't match what they'll need tomorrow.

Elijah was fortified by that food. I want you to know that God will give you the strength you need not simply to face the challenges that are right in front of you but to continue the journey that awaits. There are times when the warrior's greatest weapon is to withdraw. There are moments when if you are to advance, you must retreat. This is the profound nature of God—that when we are weak, he is strong. When we have lost our strength, he replenishes it.

Elijah's soul was starving, but God began the process of restoration by feeding his body. If you are depressed, if you are discouraged, if you've tasted the crushing blow of defeat, the most spiritual thing you can do is make sure you regain your strength. The most spiritual thing Elijah could do was eat and drink.

You are not a body with a soul; you are a soul with a body. But the health of your soul is profoundly connected to the health of your body. It doesn't sound very spiritual, but Elijah had to face the physical and emotional effects of exhaustion. He had not accounted for the toll that victory demands of the warrior. Once he had regained his strength, he then traveled for forty days and forty nights until he reached the mountain of God.

There is a journey ahead of you that will require great strength. There are many battles yet to fight. In some you will know victory, and in others you will taste defeat. But no battle will steal your life like the battle for your soul. If you are not careful, fear will drive you to run for your life and run from your life. Even when we run, God has an amazing way of meeting us as we hide in our own wilderness, helping us restore our strength and calling us back to himself.

When You've Lost Your Way

I'm always intrigued by the questions God asks his people. After Adam and Eve had eaten from the forbidden tree, God asked, "Where are you?"[111] When Elijah came to the mountain, he went into a cave and spent the night there. God asked Elijah the most fascinating question. After Elijah had run away for forty days and forty nights to a place he had never intended to go, the Lord asked him, "What are you doing here, Elijah?"[112]

At first glance it would seem that Elijah was running from Jezebel, but a more careful look at Elijah's inner turmoil makes it clear he was running from God. This understanding presses us against one of the most perplexing truths in our spiritual journeys: when you are running from your fears, you are running from God. Hidden in your fears is the faith you are searching for. If you want to meet God, stand in your fears. Stand in your pain. Stand when everything inside you tells you to withdraw. Elijah ran from God and ran right into him.

By the way, if you're running from God, he's already waiting for you, wherever your journey takes you. No matter how far you run, he will be just as close to you as he was when you left.

I don't know why we try to answer God's questions as if he doesn't already know the answer. Elijah began with a long explanation for why running for his life made perfect sense. He began by telling God everything he had done, and maybe that's part of the problem. Elijah had taken the story of God with Elijah and turned it into the story of Elijah with God. My story is not the story of me with God; it is the story of God with me. Even when I have chosen to run, God has stuck with me. When I chose to hide, God found me. When I wanted to end my life, God gave me life.

Elijah's summary of his dilemma presents a false view of reality: "I am the only one left."[113] How strange that we think we are alone when God is with us. One of our greatest fears is abandonment.

Nothing will steal your hope as powerfully as an overwhelming sense of aloneness. There are times when you will choose to walk with God and you will feel as if you are walking alone. Yet you must not forget that you are never alone: God is always with you.

God instructed Elijah to go stand on the mountain in order to encounter his presence. The Lord himself was about to pass by that very mountain: "Then a great and powerful wind tore the mountains apart and shattered the rocks before the LORD, but the LORD was not in the wind. After the wind there was an earthquake, but the LORD was not in the earthquake. After the earthquake came a fire, but the LORD was not in the fire."[114] Finally, after the fire there came "a still small voice."[115]

The way God chose to reveal himself was a reminder to Elijah that his strength was not rooted in the spectacular but in the intimate. Elijah had seen God in the wind and had seen him shake the earth and had seen him send fire from heaven. But he had forgotten that God was not in the wind or the shaking or the fire: he was in the still small voice that spoke to the depth of Elijah's soul and let him know that God was with him.

Elijah pulled his cloak over his face and stood at the mouth of the cave. Even though Elijah knew he had been found out, he covered his face to both hide from God and hide from himself. He heard the voice of the Lord once again asking him, "Elijah, what are you doing here?"[116]

Whether you are running to the battle or running from it, whether you are running for your life or running from it, never forget that the warrior's strength is not in how powerfully they can strike their sword or wield their weapon. The way of the warrior is the way of the whisper. The warrior knows who God is and who they are. Even in those moments when you find yourself struggling with discouragement or even drowning in a deep sense of despair, even in those moments when you are afraid and feel yourself past the brink of exhaustion, rather than asking God to take your life, ask him to give you life.

The Inescapable Battle

Perhaps no one knew the exhilaration of great victories better than David, who ultimately became the king of Israel. We know the stories of his great exploits, his great conquests, and his great battles. He had accomplished many mighty deeds, yet perhaps he is most frequently remembered for one of his most prominent moments of disgrace. David, at the height of his power, betrayed one of his best friends, one of his own commanders, so that he could steal his loyal friend's wife. Let that sink in for a moment. David had one of his most honorable and trustworthy leaders essentially assassinated so he could take for himself that warrior's wife.

At this time, King David had an endless number of wives and concubines. Uriah, David's commander, was an honest and courageous warrior with one wife, named Bathsheba. She was beautiful. And on one particular evening, David happened to get out of bed and walk on the roof of his palace, when he saw her bathing.

David had a choice to make. There were no Philistines to fight in that moment. There were no giants to slay from the safety of his palace. But war raged within David's soul. His present battle was the battle with the darkness within. Almost in a casual way, the story of Bathsheba begins with what may seem like an innocuous description: "In the spring, at the time when kings go off to war, David sent Joab out with the king's men and the whole Israelite army. . . . But David remained in Jerusalem."[117]

I imagine that David had no small part in the writing of his life's story. Kings often secure their legend and legacy by closely supervising the crafting of the words that recount the story of their lives. This leads me to believe that David would've been aware of the importance of that seemingly harmless line. Where Elijah ran from the battle, David simply hung back when he should have moved forward. It's a poetic description of that time of year: "in the spring, at the time when kings go off to war." Although it is beautiful, it is also profound. The story's author, Samuel, wanted his readers to understand that there was a battle that David should have been fighting but that he had abdicated his responsibility to lead. He kept the title of king but gave someone else the position's wartime responsibilities.

One of the most dangerous places to stand is where you were never supposed to be in the first place. David never should have been walking on the roof of the palace that spring evening. It was spring, and that's when kings go to war. It was spring, and David was king over Israel. It was spring, and the king's men were in the heat of battle. It was spring, and everything was happening as it should, except that David remained behind.

I wonder how often we find ourselves making our worst choices because we have abdicated the battles we are supposed to be in and then end up in battles we were never supposed to fight. David had lost his intention, and when you lose your intention, you are vulnerable to your worst decisions. In avoiding the danger of battle, David had become a liar, an adulterer, and a murderer. I have to believe that if he had seen where the last domino would fall, he never would have made that first choice.

It's often the first choice that doesn't look like a choice. The choice is clear when you choose to kill. The choice is clear when you choose to commit adultery. The choice is clear when you've chosen to look where you shouldn't have. David found out that it's hard to deny the reality of those choices. Given enough time, the evidence usually demands a verdict. What can't be seen is what is imperceptible to others and often even to ourselves. It's that first choice—the one where David decided not to go to war, the one where he chose to abdicate his responsibility, the one where he simply decided to stay behind. When you are not who you are supposed to be, you will most certainly be where you wish you had not gone. What Goliath could not do to David, complacency destroyed with ease. I am convinced that the question of the angel of the Lord for Elijah is one that God is still asking us all: "What are you doing here?" It was spring, and David should have been off to war, but instead he lost the battle to the darkness within.

You Can't Outrun the Darkness

As children we seem naturally inclined to be afraid of the dark. It's so difficult to convince a child that there's nothing in the darkness to be afraid of—that everything they outwardly fear is a projection of their inner fears. As a parent I quickly learned that all the proper explanations did not help my children at all. Only two things could help them overcome their fear. One was to turn on the light. It worked every time. The moment the light expelled the darkness, the fear was gone—until I turned the light off again. The only other solution for their fear of the dark was if I agreed to stay until they fell asleep. More often than not, I was happy to do so.

Sometimes I wonder if children are more perceptive than adults. We ignore the darkness until it consumes us. Each of us will fight the darkness within. For one of us it will be fear, for another greed. For one of us it may be despair, for another bitterness. The darkness may want you to take what is not yours or surrender what should be yours. Whether you find yourself like Elijah, overwhelmed by fear, or like David, consumed by lust, there is only one way to deal with the darkness: keep God close and become the light. The one thing you do not want to do is face the darkness alone.

When Elijah the prophet faced his dark night of the soul, he ran for his life and struggled alone in the desert. When David the king faced his darkest hour, he sent his men away and found himself alone on the roof. Not even prophets or kings should attempt to face their darkest moments alone. Not even Jesus wanted to do that.

Before Jesus allowed himself to be taken to the cross, he faced his darkest night. He often went to the Mount of Olives, which seemed to be one of his favorite places to withdraw and pray. This night was different. This time he would prepare to face the moment for which he was born. He knew what was ahead of him. He would face the brutality of the cross, and if that were not enough, he would also carry upon himself the weight of the world. The multitudes saw his suffering on the cross, but only those closest to him saw his suffering in the garden.

Jesus experienced his dark night of the soul in the Garden of Gethsemane. If anyone could face one's darkest moment alone, we would naturally assume it should have been Jesus. However, he chose to take three of his closest friends with him. He trusted Peter and John and James to know the depth of his own struggle. He asked them to wait with him as he prayed. He also asked them to pray for him and themselves. In a moment of unexpected and breathtaking transparency, Jesus said to them, "My soul is overwhelmed with sorrow to the point of death. Stay here and keep watch with me."[118]

Never Alone

One of the great lies that the darkness tells us is that we are alone. We convince ourselves that no one else has ever been through what we're facing. We believe that no one could possibly understand our pain or our sorrow. When you find yourself drowning in a deep sense of hopelessness, when with every breath you breathe you seem to only be consumed with despair, never forget there is one that not only understands but has stood where you are standing right now.

Our darkest moments rarely come because we have failed or lost a great battle; our deepest wounds come when we feel betrayed by a kiss. This is why the warrior must always guard their heart. This is where the darkness finds its way to steal your light. This is the battle that can be fought only in prayer—to respond to hate with love, to betrayal with forgiveness, to despair with hope, to darkness with light. When you need to run, don't run from God; run to him. Don't run from the people you need in your life; run to them.

Life was never meant to be lived alone. The greatest battles demand an army. You are never stronger than when standing between two warriors. It is too easy to run when you convince yourself you are the only one. It is too easy to surrender if you are fighting for only yourself. Never forget that there are no victories won without others, so why would you ever want to face defeat alone?

When you run from the battles you must fight, eventually your journey will take you full circle back to them. There are battles you must fight, wounds you must bear, and scars you must carry. To run from the battle is simply to delay the inevitable. It's not that God callously insists that you face another struggle; it's that God refuses to allow you to surrender to a lesser life than the one you were created to live.

Elijah ran because Jezebel threatened his life. The only way out that he could see was to ask God to end his life. Yet when he heard God ask him, "What are you doing here, Elijah?" he soon found himself facing the very darkness that he'd run from. There was only one way forward for Elijah; it was to return to face what he had run from—to face his fears. How else would he ever know that God would meet him in his darkest moments?

Moses was born in Egypt. It is too great of a coincidence to assume that he was raised and educated in the wisdom of the Egyptians by accident, too preposterous to believe that it was unintentional that he was raised as a son to Pharaoh, at the side of the son of Pharaoh. Everything Pharaoh knew, Moses had learned as well. All that Moses would face one day, God had prepared him for long before. Yet when it was time for Moses to face his battle, he ran for his life. In truth, he ran from his life. For forty years he ran. For forty years he ran in the wrong direction, until God encountered him and sent him back to where it all began.

Run Toward Your Future

When I first met Angela Davis, I knew she was a force of nature. She filled the room with both gentleness and confidence, with both humility and charisma. When I met her husband, Jerome, it felt as though he was the calm in the middle of the storm. He carries the meekness of harnessed power. There is a steadiness and strength to him, a magnetic kindness.

You would never know that his wife, Angela, a woman who

heals so many others, has also known deep wounds. Angela was always an athlete. She is the daughter of a former professional baseball player, so she came by her talent naturally. From the age of five until the age of eighteen, Angela was a standout soccer player, but in her senior year, she lost her love for the sport and pivoted her focus and energy to running. In her sophomore year of college, she met another athlete and was married at the age of twenty-one.

Her marriage failed, and at the age of twenty-five, she found herself divorced and a single mother of two. After the birth of her second child, she battled postpartum depression. In the midst of that dark season, she realized that her depression could be overcome only if she once again found the courage to pursue her dreams. Angela realized that when she had lost her purpose, she lost her drive. She remembered that at one time in her life her purpose was to run. This is where she regained her purpose and found God's pleasure again.

Angela could run, and she could run fast. All the way through middle school, she had always been the fastest runner in the entire school, before finally being beaten by a boy. She ran for five years as a college athlete and then pursued running professionally after her graduation. Her dad found her the best coach in Chicago.

When Angela competed to qualify for the US Olympic team, she was the twenty-fifth-fastest female runner in the world. If she'd started training as a young girl, who knows what world titles she would have attained. In the summer of 2000, Angela and Jerome connected after having met briefly years earlier. Jerome was also an athlete aspiring to make the Olympic team. Despite all their talent and hard work, neither of them made the team, and they bonded as they consoled each other. Heartache drew them together.

It was four years later when Angela was competing, fully prepared to fulfill her Olympic dreams, that she suffered an injury that ended her hopes once again. That Achilles tendon injury may have ended her career as a runner, but she never lost what she had gained.

Years before, after her divorce, Angela's dad had said to her, "You need to run to your healing." She knew the only way she would get through the divorce and all the pain she had to bear was by serving others. She knew her healing could not be found in running from her purpose but by running toward it. Angela bears the wounds of a warrior. She is marked by scars of failure, disappointment, and pain. Yet they are beautiful scars, for they mark where healing has been found.

"It was a disappointment to not make the 2000 Olympics. If I raced my best, I would have made the team," Angela said. Angela was driven by a deeply personal motivation to push herself beyond the limits of an ordinary athlete and press through the boundaries of her pain. She explained, "I wasn't running to eat; I was running to be healed." This is why we all should run.

Here in Los Angeles, Angela Davis is the envy of all those around her. She has achieved a level of celebrity and success that most only dream of. It would be easy for her to create a facade where no one could ever imagine the journey she has been on or the pain she has known. When she traveled across the country speaking to crowds of thousands, all people could see and experience was her talent and charisma. I asked Angela if I could share this small part of her backstory, as she is a perfect reminder of what a warrior really looks like. There has never been a warrior who did not know pain. There has never been a warrior who did not know failure. There has never been a warrior who did not know defeat. The strength of the warrior is that they stand in their pain. Angela Davis is a living reminder of that truth.

Sometimes we feel we cannot bear our wounds and do not believe that our healing can be found, so we run. The warrior knows they are wounded and broken. The warrior knows that their healing comes through their purpose. It is only when we return to our intention that we find our healing. If you have run away from the front line because you felt you could not bear one more wound or brave one more battle, it's time to run to your healing. For each of us the front line is different and simultaneously it is the same. The front line for all of us is a place where God calls us to stand, to live at our deepest level of faith, to fulfill our highest intention. There is only one way to your future, and that is forward.

Called to More

Jonah was called by God to preach to the nation of Nineveh, to call a nation defined by its own darkness to repentance, to stand in front of a pagan king to tell him to bow before the living God. Instead, Jonah ran for his life. The Bible is full of runners. Once when Jonah was on a ship in the midst of a raging storm, he told the sailors to throw him into the waters, thinking that by his death they would be spared. Strange how the same theme seems to recur in the lives of those we would call heroes of our faith.

After Jonah had been thrown into the ocean, the storm did stop, and a giant fish or perhaps a whale swallowed him. He sat in the belly of the beast for three days, and, white as a ghost, he was spewed out on land. He hid under a tree and wished he would die. He wanted to end his life because God had demonstrated mercy to the very nation he was supposed to preach repentance to. Once again, God would not have it. How quick we are to give up on God, but he refuses to give up on us.

After coming out of the belly of the beast, Jonah finally did go to Nineveh to preach repentance. The entire nation turned from its destructive ways and turned to God. This, by the way, was why Jonah never wanted to go in the first place. This is why he ran into his own wilderness to hide. This is why he ran from his destiny and his calling. He didn't want God to be as merciful and kind as he always knew God to be.

Jonah is a stark reminder of why we must win the battles within us.

We cannot give to the world what we do not have.

We cannot bring peace on earth if we do not have peace within.

We cannot create a world with justice if our hearts are filled with injustice.

We cannot bring hope to the world if our hearts are filled with despair.

We cannot give grace if all we know is judgment.

We cannot give forgiveness if our hearts are filled with bitterness.

Often people blame God for all the problems in the world, but he is the unlimited source of love and hope and peace and beauty and compassion. He would pour those into us without reservation and without limit.

Are we like Jonah, running from God and running from our intention because he is calling us to more and we have chosen to remain less? God never gave up on Jonah, even though Jonah did everything possible to run away from his opportunity to do unbelievable good. God could have used someone else. It might have been easier. But God wanted both Nineveh and Jonah to change. Jonah could see the great darkness in Nineveh, but he could not see the great darkness within himself. This story isn't simply about the salvation of Nineveh; it is about the salvation of Jonah.

The way of the warrior is a path of honor and nobility and service. The heart of the warrior flows from the endless well of faith, hope, and love. The warrior lives to fulfill God's intention that the world would reflect all that is good and beautiful and true. Is this the path you have chosen? If it is, then you are aware that the battle is always waged within.

I wonder how much of our lives we spend running in circles, running from our destiny, running from our calling, running from ourselves. I wish I could tell you that every battle you are meant to fight you are also destined to win, but I'm not so certain. There are battles we are called to step into not because victory is certain but because integrity demands it. Every wound the warrior bears is a sign of their honor. Scars that simply tell the story of violence or rage or anger are not the marks of a warrior. But when we bear the wounds of love, when we bear the wounds that come in the service of others, when we bear the wounds of fighting the great fight— these are the true marks of the warrior.

I have often been asked if I have tattoos. Most people seem surprised when I say I do not. What I have, though, marking every inch of my soul if not my body, are the wounds that have brought my healing. And I am grateful for every wound that has made a scar, for in them I have found the strength to heal the world. The warrior bears their wounds well, and the wounds they bear make them whole. Not only do the wounds of a warrior help the warrior find their own strength, but it is through their wounds that the warrior is able to give strength. The warrior heals through their wounds.

Your wounds are not your weakness; your wounds are your strength. Do not be ashamed of the scars. They are your marks of honor and courage and beauty. It was Paul who carried within him a thorn in the flesh that tormented him throughout his life. He begged God to remove it, but God did not. Through his suffering, Paul came to know that it was in his weakness that he was made strong.[119] I don't know the battles you have faced, the pain you have endured, the struggles you have encountered, but I am certain of this: they do not have to be your shame; they can be your glory.

I was recently in Mexico City and met an actor named Luis

Franco, who had achieved a level of fame in his country on a television series. He was married to a famous actress. At the same time that he expressed a public faith, the end of their marriage also went public. He was being accused by the media of turning to God only because his life was a mess. I could see he was in a lot of pain, that he still loved his wife, and that his faith was genuine. It was also an inescapable reality that his life was falling apart even while at the same time it was coming together.

I told him that his response to the media should actually be very simple: "You think I turned to God because my life is a mess, but you can't even see how right you are. You think my life is a mess from what you know. It's far more of a mess than you could ever know. In fact, if we were all honest with ourselves and each other, we're all a mess."

Maybe the best thing that each of us could do is to read and reread the stories of the great leaders, prophets, and kings God chose to use. The people we call heroes in the Bible were just humans. They were both the best of us and the worst of us. Adam and Eve messed up everything. To call Cain a mess would be a compliment. Abraham was a mess. Rahab was a mess. Moses was a mess. David was a mess. Scripture is full of people just like us who faced the same fears, the same struggles, the same battles, yet nothing disqualified them from living their most heroic lives.

The way of the warrior is not free from pain, it is not free from disappointment, and it is not free from failure. The warrior is known for courage, for honor, for integrity. Yet the warrior knows well the struggles that come with fear and self-doubt and even despair. The warrior faces their greatest adversary when they have to face themselves. The warrior knows there are no victories that are not first won within. Never forget who you are.

You are a warrior of light. Do not fear the darkness.

You are a warrior of hope. Do not fear despair.

You are a warrior of faith. Do not fear uncertainty.

You are a warrior of love. Do not fear hate.

You are a warrior of peace. Do not fear the battle within.

This is the fight of your life. This is the fight for your life. This is the way of the warrior.

Discussion Questions

Introduction: The Code of the Warrior

1. When you read that war is not the history of God but is the history of us, what stirred in your soul? Does this challenge or change your view of the Old Testament?
2. How have you seen a person's inner war become a war they fight with the world?
3. What would change in your life if you pursued inner peace?
4. What are you willing to sacrifice to win the battle of your inner world?
5. Do you believe that God is fighting for you? How have you seen him fight for you in the past? How is he fighting now for you to become the person you were created to be?

Code 1: The Warrior Fights Only for Peace

1. How have you seen worry steal your joy? How have you seen fear steal your freedom?
2. Do you know someone who has chosen to live in their past? How has that choice affected their life?
3. Think of an instance when you had to "turn the other cheek." How did you trust that God would fight for you when you chose the way of peace?
4. Look back on a situation when you chose to fight for yourself with vengeance, bitterness, or anger—do you see a missed op-

portunity for God to step in? How would choosing peace have brought about a different outcome?

5. What personal character red flags do you hide from yourself and others? How could you face your inner war with honesty and vulnerability? Whom could you turn to for support or encouragement?

Code 2: The Warrior Seeks to Become Invisible

1. When you are tempted to fight against people, how can you re-adjust your perspective to fight for them instead?
2. What "tree" are you striking with your life right now? How do you feel you were created and prepared to strike that tree?
3. How is your life positively affecting the world around you?
4. Which people in your life do you lean into so that you don't stay the same? Who holds you accountable? Who spurs you onward?

Code 3: The Warrior Finds Honor in Service

1. How have you seen great leaders in your life serve others?
2. Has your life been changed because someone chose to serve you? Give that person a call or write them a note in gratitude.
3. Which part of David's story do you resonate with most? Why?
4. Are you ambitious? How has your posture helped or hindered you in the pursuit of greatness?

Code 4: The Warrior Frees Their Mind

1. How have you seen your internal mind-set affect your external world? What does the way you see the world reveal about the way you see yourself?
2. How can you use spaces for creativity to enrich your life rather than escape from it?
3. How can you change your thought filter to let through more helpful thoughts than harmful ones?
4. What plan or commitment can you make today so your perspective is oriented toward the future and not the past?
5. Think of two important moments in your life, one when you took a step with faith and one when you took a step without faith. How did the outcomes differ?

Code 5: The Warrior Owns Defeat

1. What do you want to see change in your life and the world around you? How can you take responsibility for that change?
2. Do you place blame on others when something goes wrong? How does your response affect the possibility for change? How does it affect the people around you?
3. How can you take responsibility for changing difficult or negative realities that you didn't cause?
4. What is your relationship with risk? What is your relationship with failure? How can you find victory in choosing courage to face a challenge in your life, regardless of the outcome?

Code 6: The Warrior Harnesses Their Strength

1. What brings you energy? What steals your energy?
2. How can you change your habits or perspective to choose to fight only the battles that matter?
3. Has a negative emotion been posing as fuel in your life? How does choosing to fight from dark emotions lead you to burnout? What changes when you fight from a place of hope, peace, or love?
4. Do you use pain as a gateway to progress or as a roadblock? How?
5. Write down five things you want to be known for. Do you see those traits in the people around you?

Code 7: The Warrior Becomes One with All Things

1. How do you mark your life by God's presence rather than by a destination?
2. How do you see God moving around you in creation and the world?
3. How do you seek to become one with Christ?
4. How does having an eternal mind-set affect the way you live in the present and hope for the future?

Code 8: The Warrior Stands in Their Pain

1. Has life ever felt like more than you could bear? How did you face the darkness and bring it to light?

2. How has God given you strength to help yourself and others fight darkness?

3. How do you know if you're fighting a battle that isn't meant for you? Are you fighting a battle right now that isn't yours?

4. Think of a mistake you made and recall the events leading up to it—what was the first choice that led you down a dark path? What other choice could you have made?

5. When you have become lost in pain, what's the most effective way for you to get back to your original purpose and intention?

Acknowledgments

Most of all I want to thank my brilliant wife, Kim. You are the ultimate warrior.

To my son, Aaron; my daughter, Mariah; and her husband, Jake, who are always with me in this great fight we call life.

And to all whose names are not mentioned but will never be forgotten.

You are our tribe and we are forever grateful.

Together we walk the way of the warrior.

Forward,

Erwin Raphael McManus

Notes

1. See Ecclesiastes 3:8.
2. Job 3:25–26.
3. John 14:27.
4. Isaiah 9:7.
5. John 14:27.
6. Philippians 4:6, NASB.
7. See Philippians 4:6.
8. John 16:33.
9. Luke 1:76–79.
10. Wikipedia, s.v. "shalom," https://en.wikipedia.org/wiki/Shalom.
11. Philippians 4:6, NASB.
12. Isaiah 26:3.
13. Luke 1:79.
14. Luke 2:14.
15. Matthew 5:40.
16. Matthew 5:41.
17. Matthew 5:39.
18. See Matthew 21:12; Mark 11:15; John 2:15.
19. See Matthew 24:6; Mark 13:7.
20. Erwin Raphael McManus, *Uprising: A Revolution of the Soul* (Nashville: Thomas Nelson, 2010), 230.
21. Ecclesiastes 9:13–18.
22. Ecclesiastes 10:10.
23. Psalm 111:10.
24. 1 John 4:18, NASB.
25. Proverbs 27:17.

26. See Proverbs 27:5–6.

27. Ecclesiastes 4:9–12.

28. See Mark 9:33–34.

29. Mark 9:35.

30. See Matthew 20:20–21.

31. Mark 3:17.

32. Matthew 20:22.

33. Matthew 20:25–26.

34. Matthew 20:26; Mark 10:43.

35. 1 Corinthians 10:31.

36. Matthew 20:27.

37. Matthew 20:28.

38. See Mark 12:30.

39. See John 5:19, 30.

40. See John 13:2.

41. John 13:3.

42. See John 13:4–5.

43. John 13:8.

44. 1 Samuel 17:33.

45. 1 Samuel 17:34.

46. 1 Samuel 17:34–35.

47. 1 Samuel 17:36–37.

48. See 1 Samuel 17:34–35.

49. Matthew 20:26; Mark 10:43.

50. Philippians 2:3–4.

51. Online Etymology Dictionary, s.v. "memory," www.ety
monline.com/word/memory.

52. Laboratory of Neuro Imaging, "Education Brain Trivia," http://web.
archive.org/web/20170313053429/http://loni
.usc.edu/about_loni/education/brain_trivia.php.

53. "80% of Thoughts Are Negative . . . 95% Are Repetitive," *The*

Miracle Zone (blog), March 2, 2012, https://faith
hopeandpsychology.wordpress.com/2012/03/02/80-of
-thoughts-are-negative-95-are-repetitive/.

54. Romans 12:2.

55. See Romans 12:2.

56. See Hebrews 11:1.

57. See Genesis 2:15–17.

58. Genesis 3:10.

59. Genesis 3:11.

60. Genesis 3:12.

61. Genesis 3:13.

62. Genesis 3:13.

63. See Matthew 25:14–30, NASB.

64. See "Talent Conversion Chart," Convert-me.com, https://
m.convert-me.com/en/convert/history_weight/bibtalent.
html?u=bibtalent&v=1; Mary Fairchild, "How Heavy Was
a Talent in the Bible? A Talent Was an Ancient Measurement for
Weighing Gold and Silver," ThoughtCo., March 17, 2018, www.
thoughtco.com/what-is-a-talent-700699.

65. It's an approximate number. It will be dependent on the current price
of gold.

66. Matthew 25:24.

67. See Matthew 25:25.

68. Cristina Lapenna, "5 Reasons Why Your Watch Stopped Working,"
The Long's Blog, October 19, 2015, https://blog
.longsjewelers.com/watches/watch-stopped-working; Sunson
505, "Why Wrist Watches Stop Working on Some People," *ieboturk-
son99* (blog), May 8, 2013, https://ieboturkson99
.wordpress.com/2013/05/08/why-wrist-watches-stop-working
-on-some-people/.

69. *Encyclopedia Britannica,* s.v. "Special Relativity," www

.britannica.com/science/special-relativity; *Encyclopedia Britannica,*
s.v. "Relativity," by Sidney Perkowitz, www
.britannica.com/science/relativity.

70. See Nehemiah 8:10.

71. James 1:6–8.

72. Adapted from philosophers John Stuart Mill and Edmund Burke,
"The Only Thing Necessary for the Triumph of Evil Is That Good
Men Do Nothing," Quote Investigator, https://quoteinvestigator.
com/2010/12/04/good-men-do/.

73. Isaiah 40:29–31.

74. See John 10:10.

75. See Mark 5:30–31.

76. See John 5:19, 30.

77. 2 Corinthians 12:9.

78. See 2 Corinthians 12:9.

79. Genesis 1:3.

80. See Jeremiah 20:9.

81. James 1:17.

82. Paulo Coelho, *The Alchemist,* trans. Alan R. Clarke (New York:
HarperCollins, 2006), 36.

83. See Acts 17:28.

84. See James 5:17.

85. See 1 Kings 18.

86. See 1 Kings 18:42–44.

87. See Ezekiel 37:1–14.

88. John 20:21.

89. John 20:22.

90. Genesis 1:3.

91. Genesis 2:7.

92. See Matthew 14:28.

93. See Matthew 14:30.

94. See John 17:11.

95. See James 5:17.

96. Colossians 1:15–20.

97. Hebrews 11:6.

98. See Hebrews 11:1.

99. Hebrews 11:3.

100. This story is also in my book *The Barbarian Way: Unleash the Untamed Faith Within* (Nashville: Thomas Nelson, 2005), 72–77. Used with permission of Thomas Nelson, www.thomasnelson.com.

101. Genesis 5:24.

102. Ecclesiastes 3:11.

103. Matthew 16:19; 18:18.

104. See 1 Kings 18.

105. 1 Kings 18:27.

106. 1 Kings 18:39.

107. See 1 Kings 19:2.

108. 1 Kings 19:3.

109. 1 Kings 19:4–5.

110. 1 Kings 19:7.

111. Genesis 3:9.

112. 1 Kings 19:9.

113. 1 Kings 19:10.

114. 1 Kings 19:11–12.

115. 1 Kings 19:12, KJV.

116. See 1 Kings 19:13.

117. 2 Samuel 11:1.

118. Matthew 26:38.

119. See 2 Corinthians 12:7–10